TEXAS STORIES

I Like to Tell My Friends

TEXAS STORIES

I Like to Tell My Friends

Real-life Tales of Love, Betrayal, and Dreams
from the History of the Lone Star State

T. Lindsay Baker

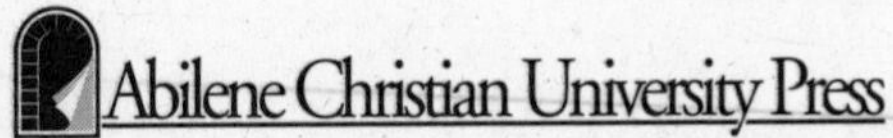

TEXAS STORIES I LIKE TO TELL MY FRIENDS

REAL-LIFE TALES OF LOVE, BETRAYAL, AND DREAMS FROM THE HISTORY OF THE LONE STAR STATE

ACU PRESS

ISBN 978-0-89112-268-5
LCCN 2011010198

Printed in the United States of America

Cover photo image courtesy of Fort Concho National Historic Landmark. Used by permission.

Internal images of Texas locations hand-drawn by and courtesy of Don Collins. Images taken from *Traces of Forgotten Places* (TCU Press, 2008) by Don Collins. Used by permission.

Texas Region Map provided by Dr. Charles Grear. Used by permission.

LIBRARY OF CONGRESS CATALOGING-IN-PUBLICATION DATA
Baker, T. Lindsay.
Texas stories I like to tell my friends : real-life tales of love, betrayal, and dreams from the history of the Lone Star State / by T. Lindsay Baker.
p. cm.
ISBN 978-0-89112-268-5
1. Texas--History--Anecdotes. 2. Texas--History, Local--Anecdotes. 3. Texas--Biography--Anecdotes. 4. Tales--Texas. I. Title.
F386.6.B35 2011
976.4--dc22

2011010198

Cover design by MTWdesign
Interior text design by Sandy Armstrong

For information contact:
Abilene Christian University Press
1626 Campus Court
Abilene, Texas 79601

1-877-816-4455
www.abilenechristianuniversitypress.com

11 12 13 14 15 16 / 7 6 5 4 3 2 1

To Julie, who patiently listens to my stories even when she tires of them.

Texas Region Map

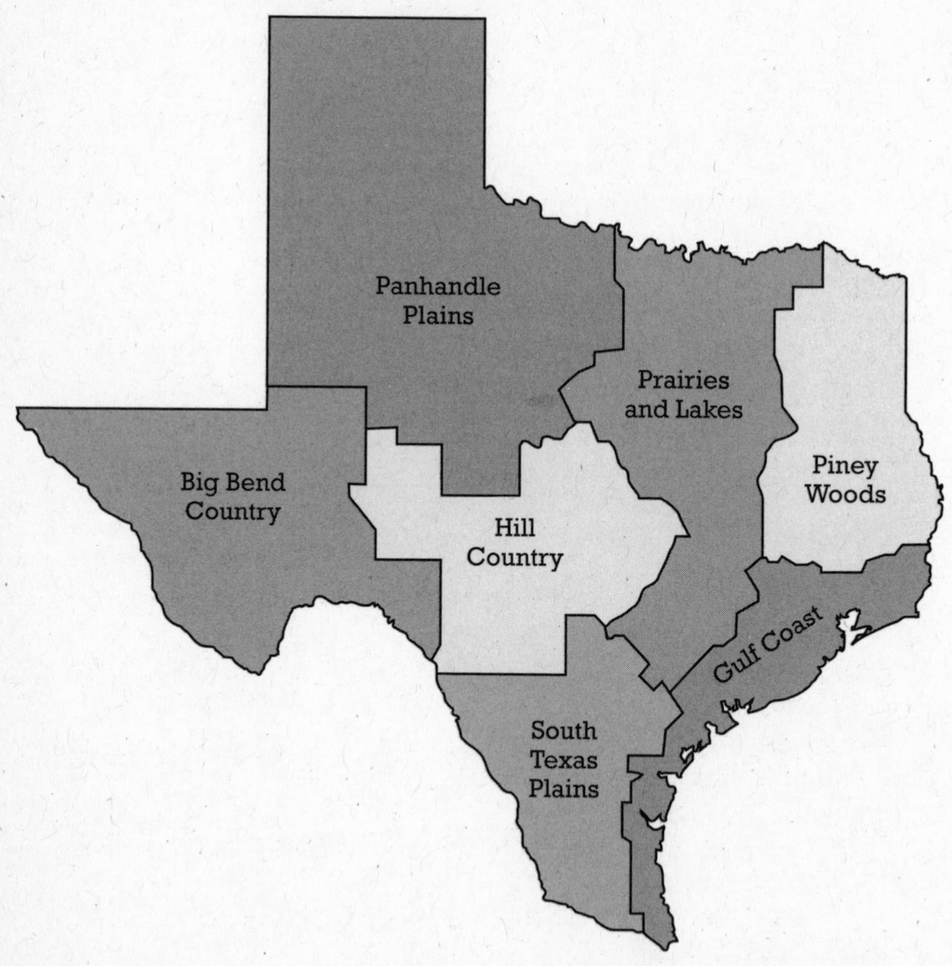

Table of Contents

III. Hill Country

IV. Panhandle Plains

V. Piney Woods

VI. Prairies and Lakes

VII. South Texas Plains

VIII. Somewhere in Texas

Foreword

For years I have enjoyed road trips with friends. My wife fears that I may bore them to death telling stories about roadside locations as we pass. The past people who once lived in these places, however, populate my life.

It is impossible for me to travel east or west on Interstate 20 without thinking about its history. The town of Cisco, for example, blossomed in the teens and twenties due to oil-based prosperity and then declined, leaving behind an impressive downtown and Conrad Hilton's first hotel. My mind then flies to church camp I attended in the 1960s just north of Cisco, and the open-air fun I had splashing around with friends in the shadow of a big concrete dam in "the world's largest swimming pool." (Later I learned that it did indeed deserve that distinction.) From the pool my thoughts come back to the town of Cisco and its most famous bungled crime in the annals of the state—the 1927 Santa Claus bank robbery. Wherever I look there seems to be yet another Texas story that merits recounting.

For years I have admired the success of historian and colleague J'Nell Pate. Since the 1980s, in a town where she lived just west of Fort Worth, she has authored a weekly history-based newspaper column for *The Azle News*. At the time, I was working at the Panhandle-Plains Historical Museum in Canyon, Texas. When I saw how much fun she had writing these features for audiences outside of her college classroom, it occurred to me that I might do the same. So, in 1987 I signed up to take a feature writing course at nearby Amarillo College. I even convinced Bill Brown—then the curator of anthropology at the museum—to join me in the classroom. The instructor taught us the basics of journalistic writing, and I started putting together a few prospective newspaper stories as class assignments. This was far from the strict scholarly writing that I had learned as a graduate student at Texas Tech. My target audience became the people I envisioned sitting beneath the awnings of filling stations whiling their time away with the local paper as they waited for customers. If my words weren't engaging, they would just flip over to the next page.

After completing the feature-writing class, I decided that I was as ready as I would ever be to start self-syndicating a Texas history newspaper column. With a mailing list from a membership directory for the Texas Press Association, I sent a month of free columns and a subscription form to scores of in-state newspapers. A few of them wrote back with money subscriptions to keep receiving the stories. Eventually the features appeared in papers from *The Clarendon Enterprise* in the Panhandle to *The Victoria Advocate* on the Texas Gulf Coast. I enjoyed writing the features for four years, but in time other duties intruded into my foray in journalism.

Since producing these stories I have applied the journalistic writing techniques that I learned to my other works as well. These were helpful lessons. Now I pen press releases and book chapters in a fraction of the time that they used to take, and I now think of my audiences in much broader terms than before. Today I know to look for intriguing human-interest stories that I can "plug into" my books and classroom lectures. I have come to realize that there are compelling stories waiting to be told behind just about every abandoned farmhouse and mesquite stump that I see alongside the road.

T. Lindsay Baker,
Rio Vista, Texas

I.

BIG BEND COUNTRY

Broad-shouldered Tom

Prospecting in far West Texas was not the healthiest thing to be doing in 1852 because the native inhabitants, the Apache Indians, resented the intrusions by any outsiders. Their resentment took the form of attacks with bows, arrows, lances, and firearms.

The dream of instant riches, however, lured Americans into the dangerous region, among them William Snyder and his slave, Tom. In summer 1852 Snyder had met James Adams, a seasoned scout and frontiersman, in San Antonio, and there they discussed tales that they had heard from old Mexicans in the city about gold in the country far to the west.

After making their plans for an expedition to the area of the Big Bend on the Rio Grande, Snyder returned home to East Texas, where he was a planter. There he adjusted his affairs for an extended absence and then returned to San Antonio with one of his most trusted slaves, a huge thirty-five-year-old black man named Tom. In the meantime Adams had recruited a fourth member to the party, a frontiersman named Lucien Daley.

The four men departed San Antonio while the weather was still hot in 1852, traveling overland to the head of the Guadalupe and then westward across the Devils River and the Pecos, turning southward toward the area of the Chisos Mountains. Daley, the only member of the party who actually knew anything about prospecting, said that he found traces of gold. They then proceeded through rough country up the Rio Grande Valley.

While prospecting in this desert country, the four men were set upon by a party of about twenty Apache Indians, into whose domain they had trespassed. "Lord, Mars William! Look yonder, coming!" Tom reputedly exclaimed as the warriors first came into view. The prospectors made for a nearby sinkhole that Adams had already spotted.

As the men ran for the depression, one of the Apaches managed a gunshot that broke William Snyder's hip, crippling him. Slave Tom dropped his gun and picked up his master, carrying him on to the sinkhole, while one of the other men retrieved the firearm.

For the next four days the men found themselves trapped in the natural depression surrounded by Apaches. During the siege the prospectors did shoot several of the attackers, but they still were trapped. Tom bemoaned the loss to the Indians of "Old Tom," the favorite mule from the plantation, which Snyder had brought along on the trip as a pack animal. Daley and Adams did most of the shooting, Tom keeping the guns loaded as best he could. They never discharged all of their guns at once, keeping two long guns and the pistols loaded all the time.

Black Tom was so greatly distressed over the loss of "Old Tom" to the Apaches, that he prevailed on the white men to let him try to shoot an Indian, though he only succeeded in shooting off a warrior's cap.

If all the men had been sound of limb, they might have tried to escape at night southward toward the Rio Grande, but Snyder's condition precluded such an attempt. Day after day, night after night, for four days they waited, caught without food or water other than the moist sand in the bottom of the sinkhole.

As the fourth day wore on, Snyder roused himself from his stupor of fever and pain to advise all the others to try to escape at night. "You who are able must get out of here and fight your way through. . . . I must stay and meet my fate. . . . I cannot stand this much longer and the sooner it is ended, the better."

By this time Tom was crying at his master's words, declaring, "Mars William, you have always been good to me. . . . I won't go off and leave you here. I'm going to stand and die with you. I'll never go back to old missus without you." To this Adams stated, "We will all leave here all together or not at all."

Snyder could not walk a step, but Tom solved that problem. Large in stature and in the prime of life, the 240-pound enslaved man volunteered to carry his master on his back while the other two men carried the firearms.

The night proved overcast and drizzly—ideal for an escape. Through the pitch-black darkness, the four men silently passed down the draw unseen by Apache sentries, the rain muffling their steps while providing them relief from thirst. When morning came it was foggy, providing additional time to retreat from the attackers.

Frequent stops had to be made for Tom to rest, but he tenderly carried Snyder all the way to the Rio Grande where the party stopped long enough to hunt some game and cook a meal. Tom continued to assure Snyder that all they had to do was to follow Adams and that he would "get 'em all out of this scrape."

Strengthened by food and water, they continued on to the copper mines on the Conchos River in northern Mexico, where they were well treated by the inhabitants until Snyder recovered enough to make it on to San Antonio by way of Fort Clark and Fort Inge.

On return to East Texas, Tom reportedly never tired of telling the story of his big battle with the "'Pache Indians," always winding up with his regrets over the loss of "Old Tom," the mule.

The Guadalupe Pass Club

I like to think that there's a sort of club. It consists of the people who have been over the Guadalupe Pass out west of the Pecos and just south of the New Mexico line.

One of the early "members" of this club was Waterman L. Ormsby. When you read what he had to say about his approach to the Guadalupe Mountains from the east, you begin to see what I mean. "The Guadalupe Peak loomed up before us all day in the most aggravating manner. It fairly seemed to be further off the more we traveled." If you've driven Ranch Road 652 westward from Orla, a little south of Ormsby's route, you understand what he was talking about.

Ormsby described the mountains as he saw them on September 28, 1858. At the time, he was the only through passenger on the first westbound stage of the Butterfield Overland Mail. The route connected St. Louis on the Mississippi with San Francisco on the Pacific, about 2,800 miles by stagecoach.

The trip over the Guadalupe Pass was a high point both in elevation and in experience for Ormsby during his transcontinental journey. Fortunately for us, he was a journalist. As such, he documented his trip in installments for his employer, the *New York Herald*, and on

November 11, 1858, the paper carried a report of his trip across Trans-Pecos Texas.

For over a day, Ormsby watched the Guadalupe Mountains gradually draw nearer as he bounced across the plains approaching the Pecos River. On September 27 he wrote, "As we neared Pope's Camp, in the bright moonlight, we could see the Guadalupe Mountains, sixty miles distant on the other side of the river, standing out in bold relief against the clear sky, like walls of some ancient fortress covered with towers and battlements."

"I am told," he went on to explain, "that on a clear day this peak has been seen across the plains for the distance of one hundred miles, so tall is it and so low the country about it." Those of us who are "members" of the club can understand.

The route to the Pinery stagecoach station at the crest of the Guadalupe Pass, over fifty-six hundred feet in elevation, was exceedingly steep and rough; the stagecoach mules balking all the way. Ormsby complained, "We were obliged actually to beat our mules with rocks to make them go the remaining five miles to the station." The track was one of the roughest that Ormsby found on the trip. "The road winds over some of the steepest and stoniest hills I had yet seen, studded with inextricable rocks, each of which seems ready to jolt the wagon into the abyss below."

Once they reached the stage stop at the crest of the pass, Ormsby found a rock-walled station building with a tall picket corral in the mouth of Pine Canyon. Its ruins are still there, protected within the Guadalupe Mountains National Park. The park service even provides a printed brochure that helps modern visitors identify the various rooms.

Above all stand the mountains. To Ormsby they seemed beautiful but ominous. "The great peak towers as if ready at any moment to fall, while huge boulders hang as if ready, with the weight of a rain drop, to be loosened from their fastenings and descend with lumbering swiftness to the bottom, carrying destruction in their paths."

Despite the mountain grandeur all about him, Waterman Ormsby was even more impressed by his views of the heavens. "I shall never forget the gorgeous appearance of the clouds, tinged by the setting sun above those jagged peaks, changing like a rapid panorama," he wrote in awe. "They assumed all sorts of fantastic shapes, from frantic maidens with dishevelled hair to huge monsters of fierce demeanor, chasing one another through the realms of space."

Any club member who also has crossed the Guadalupe Pass and who too has marveled at its wild beauty must acknowledge that Waterman L. Ormsby be counted as a charter member of our non-exclusive club.

The Surveyor and the Polecat

We are in the season for summer thunderstorms, and it was one of these downpours which unexpectedly brought land surveyor Oscar Williams into uncomfortably close contact with a polecat in the 1880s.

The scent from the skunk is both very strong and very persistent. The yellowish liquid has such a long-lasting odor that even after a person who has been sprayed can no longer sense it, strangers detect the scent immediately.

The summer downpour that drenched Oscar Williams and his surveying crew on the Llano Estacado of West Texas also created a number of instant streams flowing through the gulleys in the vicinity. Some of these small water-filled draws ran through a prairie dog town, and the young men on the expedition saw this as an opportunity for catching some of its burrowing residents.

They set to work with mattocks and spades to excavate channels from the arroyos to carry the muddy waters into the prairie dog holes. "As the water rose in the hole, the dog came with it and was easily caught," Williams later reported in a story published about 1908 in the Fort Stockton paper.

Oscar Williams, however, found more than his expected prairie dog. "I had 'drowned out' an unusually vigorous customer, but he had escaped me and taken down into a neighboring hole," he wrote. The surveyor followed the animal to the second burrow, trenching floodwaters to it as well and hoping to force the critter out of his second retreat.

"I waited for the proper time to lift up the spade and catch the dog," Williams said. "This had been our successful practice, so one can imagine my surprise when I lifted my spade to find, not a half-drowned prairie dog but a full grown and very unfriendly skunk."

Emerging from the burrow "bristled up," the black-and-white cousin of the weasel turned its rear toward the unsuspecting Williams and let loose a well-directed spray of scent.

This problem sounds bad, but it was not the worst part for Williams. The surveyors had been in the field longer than they had expected, and all the men had grown short of clothes. "Socks, shoes, pants, shirts and other clothes had worn out or had been discarded until no one had a garment in reserve," Williams remembered. This meant that the poor man could not change out of his malodorous garments.

Surveyor Williams tried everything that he and his friends could think of to remove the odor. After finding that washing in soapy water did little good, he next tried taking off his clothes at bedtime and burying them in the ground overnight.

It was all to no avail. "I became a sort of pariah among my own people," he wrote, noting that he could not even eat with his friends due to his objectionable odor.

"In time it came about that I failed to notice the odor, but wherever I went the others respectfully gave way," Williams recalled. "I used to lay awake at night studying how to get rid of my companion, the odor," he said. Occasionally he repeated to himself the verse from a poet:

"You may break, you may shatter the vase if you will, / But the scent of the roses will hang 'round it still."

The only difference for Oscar Williams was that the scent didn't come from roses, but rather from the polecat.

After suffering the ill effects of his encounter with the skunk for three weeks, Williams and his fellow surveyors found their way to a frontier store. There Williams finally was able to buy new, clean clothes. Observing the storekeeper, Williams noted, "I was much disposed to suspect from the twitching of the merchant's nostrils while he sold me my outfit that the scent of the roses hung 'round me still, at the end of the three weeks."

Beaver Trapper of Del Rio

By the 1920s Jim McMahon of Del Rio was known as "the Old Man of the River," for he had been living along the banks of the Rio Grande since 1874. His livelihood, to the surprise of many, was that of a beaver trapper. The Rio Grande flowed through arid country with few trees, so it did not present what most people would consider to be a habitat for beavers.

McMahon, a native of Tennessee, came to Texas as a boy about 1857, relocating westward as the frontier moved that direction. He was twenty-nine years old when he first camped on the Rio Grande, and he remembered it well:

"It was right here near where Del Rio is," he told a reporter from the *Dearborn Independent*. "The moon was shining on the river and the stars were big and grand. I was moseying along the bank when I saw a fat, shiny beaver push out for midstream to head off a floating log." That very night he observed thirty beavers, "purty things, sleek and brown," he remembered. "I decided then to be a trapper—and I've been one ever since, right on this river."

According to McMahon, the coming of the Southern Pacific Railroad in 1881 "at one stroke" civilized the "border frontier" along its route, but even so the country back from the steel rails remained wild. Three years after the coming of the railway, in December 1884, he and another trapper nearly met their deaths in this "wild" area and in the process became perhaps the first recorded men to pass by boat through all of the Santa Helena, Mariscal, and Boquillas Canyons of the Rio Grande.

McMahon and companion Willis Pafford had set out beaver trapping, but bandits from south of the border changed their plans. "They chased us from Presidio to the shut-in of the first canyon, Santa Helena," he stated.

Realizing that they were caught with only the canyons as an escape route, the two men set off in their two-hundred-fifty-pound cypress boat through the gorge of Santa Helena. All the time the robbers followed along the canyon tops "and shot at us as we came through."

Along the way they discovered the body of another trapper who had been killed a few days before. "He was lying on a sand bar, shot to pieces, rotting in the sun," he said.

McMahon and Pafford made it through all three canyons in fifteen days, which remained for years the fastest passage recorded. Even so, it was not easy going. "The boat turned over four or five times and we was always portaging it over boulders fallen from the cliffs," he noted. Because of the height to which they had to lift the boat, it took them three days to get around just one huge rock. Afterward "when we dropped into the current," he related, "it whirled us along like a train for the next five miles."

When the reporter in 1925 asked Jim McMahon what had made his life worth living, the old man thought and responded that true happiness could come only to those who lived among wild things. His own life's passion came from association with the furred, finned, and feathered creatures of the river, even though he ironically made his living by snaring them.

McMahon's fur buyer in St. Louis declared him to be "the world's champion beaver trapper," for every year from 1874 to 1925 he had averaged a season's catch of 150 beavers—in a land generally considered to be beaver poor.

II.

GULF COAST

As Content as Could Be Expected

Twenty-three-year-old Moses Lapham came to Texas in 1831 and stayed there for most of the remainder of his life, but he never really liked it very much. He apparently stayed on in the new land after discovering that he could support himself from the proceeds of part-time land surveying, spending the rest of his hours in quiet personal study and reading.

Lapham initially lived in the home of Thomas H. Borden near the Brazos River close to San Felipe, Texas. There he taught school and worked as an occasional member of Borden's land surveying crew.

Texan social life offered little appeal to college-educated Lapham, who found most people in the new country to be boors. In July 1831 he complained to his father in Ohio, "The society in town is such as to preclude all satisfaction," noting that its members' most favored pastimes were "drinking, gambling, swearing & fighting." Unlike many immigrants to Texas, Lapham found the rawness unbearable. Only in his books could he find relief.

Health concerns were significant for all residents on the Texas frontier, where even a sore tooth could represent pure misery. "I am in good health now excepting the toothache," he wrote to his father in January 1832. He had asked a local physician to try to pull the offending denticle, but he "broke it off close to the jaw-bone." With no anesthesia available to deaden the pain for further efforts at removal, the Ohioan resigned himself to the problem: "It has pained me worse since than before, but I hope it will soon rot out."

The toothache pain soon was supplanted by that in Lapham's foot. He reported home that he had been out cutting timber with Thomas Borden in January 1832. "I had not cut but two or three bushes," he wrote, "before the ax glanced off & hit my foot." The blow was a minor one, but the Ohioan had on inappropriate footwear. "My shoe being thin, it went through the leather and into the foot between the great toe and next to the great toe." The cut bled freely until Lapham stopped it with a piece of cloth that he happened to have in his pocket.

Even though temporarily disabled, the grumpy surveyor continued his reports, never becoming enamored with his new home. "Texas possesses many advantages," he wrote home, adding in the same stroke of the pen, "and many disadvantages."

Lapham noted that he had received an invitation to attend a dance held at San Felipe, but, as he reported, "I . . . declined. I had much rather spend the evening in contemplating the beauties of nature or reading than to mingle in the crowd of giddy pleasure where pride, vanity, and ignorance clad in gaudy dress is the only pinnacle of preeminence." The newcomer had very little to do with people like those at the dance in San Felipe, where "good society is exceedingly rare and morals are more corrupt than in almost any other part of the world."

Finally, ending a letter penned on February 15, 1832, Lapham perhaps best described his personal situation in Texas: "I am as contented as could be expected."

What Ladies Should Bring to Texas

"Delicate ladies find they can be useful and need not be vain," wrote Mary Austin Holley from Bolivar, Texas, in December 1831.

Mrs. Holley, a cousin of Stephen F. Austin, traveled from her home in the United States to Mexican Texas in 1831. Her reason for the trip was to inspect land on Galveston Bay on which she planned to settle. Two years later, in 1833, she published a fascinating book, *Texas*, which she based on her experiences in the new land.

In part of her 1833 book, Mrs. Holley gave advice to prospective women colonists about what belongings they should take if they chose to settle in frontier Texas.

"Housekeepers should bring with them all indispensable articles for household use," she recommended. "Ladies in particular should remember that in a new country they cannot get things made at any moment as in an old one."

Extra clothing was always good to have. Mrs. Holley advised that mothers carry along "as much clothing . . . for themselves and their children as they conveniently can." She went on to explain that in Texas ladies would be "sufficiently busy in the first two years in arranging such things as they have without occupying themselves in obtaining more."

Mrs. Holley felt that women could never bring too many household items to pioneer Texas, because extras could always be traded to other colonists for things that were needed. She explained, "If on arrival they find a surplus on hand, it can be readily disposed of to advantage." Most buying and selling was by exchange, she related. "Trade by barter is much practiced, and you can buy provisions with coffee, calico, tea-kettles, and saucepans instead of cash."

Because of its size and weight, moving furniture to Texas presented special problems for new settlers. Mrs. Holley suggested disassembling it prior to shipment. "Furniture such as chairs and bureaus can be brought in separate pieces and put together cheaper and better after arrival than they can be purchased here, if purchased at all."

According to Mrs. Holley, the concern among Texas settlers of the 1830s was not for tables, but rather "to get something to put upon them." Large amounts of furniture were not needed by the colonists anyway, Mrs. Holley explained, because "houses are small, and buildings expensive."

Summarizing her suggestions for housekeepers planning to emigrate from the United States to Texas, Mary Austin Holley advised that the maxim to follow in Texas was "nothing for show, but all for use."

A Texas Jury Decision

John Washington Lockhart, for many years a resident of the Brazos bottoms, told many tales of early days there during the middle of the nineteenth century. One of these stories dealt with the trial of "Old Phil" Claborn.

Claborn resided in Brazoria County, where a neighbor had taken into his home an orphan boy. The young man had gone there, offering the farmer to do whatever he could to pay for his keep. The farmer agreed, but whenever the boy did anything wrong, he beat him unmercifully. This situation had not gone on too long when "Old Phil" discovered what was happening. After the orphan boy sought Claborn's assistance following an especially severe beating, he had his horse saddled and rode off in haste to investigate.

By the time Claborn reached the neighbor's place, he would not accept any excuses. "Although greeted by the offender civilly," Lockhart related, "Uncle Phil was in no state of mind to hear explanation, but knocked the man down and proceeded to administer a sound thrashing to him."

The assaulted farmer pressed charges against Claborn for the attack, and in due time the court met on the matter. Claborn employed two local attorneys, W. L. Jones and Jones Rivers, to defend him. As the latter was young and already becoming known as an orator, the elder lawyer allowed him to carry the weight of Claborn's representation. During the prosecution stage of the proceedings, the judge called the farmer to show to the jury the marks of his injury inflicted by Claborn.

When the time came for the defense to speak, attorney Rivers first quoted the Bible text that each man should be a father to the fatherless and should visit the widows and orphans in their afflictions.

"Now," Rivers argued, "who is the father to this poor boy?" Then he answered his own interrogatory: "My client has done no more than he was commanded to. What father would not resent the beastly beating this poor orphan was subjected to?" The eloquent attorney continued to elaborate his position in defense of Claborn, and by the time that he was finished he reputedly had both the judge and the jury in tears.

When the judge gave the case to the jury for its decision, the foreman stood up and asked if the panel could render its verdict without leaving the courtroom. The judge assented to the request, whereupon the foreman reported, "We, the jury, find the defendant not guilty," he said, adding, "and we recommend that Phil Claborn do it again!"

Overnight at the Brazoria Hotel

Finding a room for the night in pioneer Texas was not an easy task. So discovered a New York land buyer who came to Texas in 1831, when it still was part of Mexico. Three years later, in 1834, this traveler, now anonymous, published a report of his experiences in a book he titled *A Visit to Texas.*

The only hotels the traveler found in Texas were in Brazoria and San Felipe. Because his lodging in Brazoria was "a pretty fair specimen of most of the best houses in the country," he described it for his readers in considerable detail. Today the account tells us much about travel in early Texas.

He described the building, a dogtrot cabin, in this way: "Two square houses, about fifteen feet apart, are constructed of logs, well fitted together by deep mortices cut at their ends. . . . Each of these buildings has a door in the middle on the side facing inwards, and the space between them being covered by a roof, a broad passage is left, shelter indeed above, but quite open at both ends."

The Brazoria hotel, he noted, had a fireplace at the end of each of its two rooms "and a hole through the roof for smoke." The windows, "destitute of glass," closed with wooden shutters.

The New Yorker found himself to be a source of interest among the guests at Brazoria, for he carried with him news from the outside world. He reported, "Every well behaved stranger, on account of the news he brings, is a welcome visitor in such families as these." He later wrote, "The time passed very pleasantly. . . . The company were cheerful, conversation was lively, [and] our arrival brought new subjects of attraction and inquiry to all."

The traveler was pleasantly surprised to learn that the hotel owner's wife also hailed from New York, and the connection resulted in special treatment. "Her care furnished us with excellent food considering the disadvantages of the place, while her arrangements afforded us more comfort and convenience than we could have expected in a habitation so disproportioned to our numbers."

The accommodations were indeed "disproportioned" to the number of guests, for thirty men occupied a single room—one of the two that comprised the hotel. The mattresses, probably filled with either hay or Spanish moss, lay directly on the floor. "In order to place 30 men in a horizontal position, on a space about 20 feet square, and each upon a separate bed, required no small care and calculation."

The traveler concluded his commentary on the Brazoria hotel by noting, "We laid ourselves down, as on the floor of a steamboat, and slept soundly till morning."

The Boatman's Wife of Boca Chica Creek

Teresa Griffin Viele accompanied her army officer husband to the South Texas frontier in the middle of the 1850s, recording her impressions in a journal published in 1858 as *Following the Drum*. In the work, she describes Texas as she viewed it and describes much about what it must have been like to live in the region well over a century ago.

Teresa and her husband, Egbert L. Viele, landed on Brazos Island at Brazos Santiago Harbor, located at the south end of Laguna Madre just north of the Rio Grande mouth in extreme South Texas. The nearest modern-day town is Port Isabel. "Brazos Island looks like a bleak, barren sandbank on a pretty extensive scale," she noted in her journal. Today part of it forms the Brazos Island State Park, and its appearance hasn't changed very much.

The officer's wife observed that the population on the island consisted principally of army personnel working at large quartermaster department warehouses and a handful of fishermen "who supply the Brownsville market with bass, red and blue-fish." She noted that the fishermen also gathered what she termed "an inferior kind of Oyster" that was "regarded as a very great delicacy in the absence of others."

After spending the night at Brazos Island, Mrs. Viele and her husband were met by an army carriage to transport them to Fort Brown at Brownsville. The first part of the trip stretched along the beachfront of Brazos Island, where the party saw "no rocks, nor the smallest traces of vegetation." Nothing varied the monotony except "vestiges of wrecks of all descriptions." The driver had to turn aside several times just to get some of the larger pieces of the former vessels.

At Boca Chica Creek the travelers crossed flood-swollen waters from Brazos Island on a flatboat that served as a ferry. First it drew the carriage across, followed by the horses, and finally by the passengers. Since the stream had flooded out of its banks, the boat could approach within only about twenty yards of the people on the shore. "To my amazement," Mrs. Viele reported, "I soon found myself being borne through the air like a baby in the arms of a great stalwart Texan [he being knee-deep in the water], until safely lodged on the boat, on a large Mexican poncho that their galantry had provided." She was impressed.

Once across the creek, the party retired to the boatman's house, the only shelter for miles around. To Mrs. Viele, it appeared to be in a very lonesome setting with only sand and water in sight, but the interior of the house was "quite spacious" and "was divided into apartments by rough canvas or sailcloth curtains."

Visiting with the boatman's wife, Teresa learned that she had grown up on the canals of the northeastern states but had lived in all parts of the West "and had finally reached this barren spot, on the confines of civilization." To Mrs. Viele, "She bore the traces of some former beauty," but "her eyes were very sad, and so was her smile." Replying to a question about loneliness, the boatman's wife responded that all she sought at that point in her life was peace, and that she had found it at Boca Chica Creek.

The woman told Mrs. Viele that she found her chief occupation in raising chickens for the Brownsville market. The guest had noted that no chickens had been visible outside the house, though their signs were there. "She showed me a brood of fifty, with one old hen, all crowded in a bandbox, and kept on a shelf." Explaining her unusual poultry raising methods, the woman told Teresa that the close confinement kept the birds "from running in the creek." Through the application of plenty of meal but little sunlight, the boatman's wife declared that she raised the fattest chickens in the market.

"By the time that the investigation of this natural phenomenon was finished," Mrs. Viele said, "our horses were rested and at the door waiting for us."

She was off to find more adventures.

The Loss of the Mignonette

It's not very often that people think about lighthouses on the Texas Gulf Coast, and even less often do they consider the ships that took care of them. Texas certainly had both, and the sinking of one of the maintenance tenders off the mouth of the Rio Grande in 1887 constituted one of the greatest lighthouse related disasters on the entire Gulf Coast.

The area at the mouth of the Rio Grande a century ago was served by the harbor just inside Brazos Santiago Pass, the gap between the south tip of Padre Island and the much smaller Brazos Island. The reason for this situation was that the Rio Grande mouth itself was too shallow to serve as a harbor. The bay at the south end of Laguna Madre behind Padre Island could accommodate only comparatively small vessels, but even so it became the port that served all of the Rio Grande Valley of both Texas and Mexico.

In the early 1850s the U.S. Treasury Department established two lighthouses to guide mariners into this harbor, one called Brazos Santiago at the south tip of Padre Island and the other called Point Isabel Lighthouse at what today is the port town of Port Isabel. From time to time lighthouse tenders sailed to the Brazos Santiago area to undertake repairs to the light stations, as occurred on September 15, 1887, when the schooner *Mignonette* dropped anchor near the Brazos Santiago Lighthouse to repair leaks in its roof.

The wooden sailing vessel with its sixteen-man crew and work force had been at Brazos Santiago less than a week when a tropical storm began brewing. Every person on board knew that the ship was in an area that provided only an insecure anchorage at best during hurricane season, and that was just when they were there.

On the morning of September 21, 1887, winds and waves wrenched the schooner *Mignonette* from its moorings and swept it to sea, unseen by anyone ashore. The best supposition by Lighthouse Service officials was that the ship dragged its anchor, ran adrift before the winds, and struck its bottom on the sandbar at the entrance to Brazos Santiago Pass, ripping the hull open. From that point the ship was swept farther into the deep water to founder.

Lighthouse Engineer William H. Heuer from New Orleans telegraphed to the Lighthouse Board in Washington the message: "Mignonette dragged to sea over Brazos Bar during gale on twenty-first, nothing seen or heard since." Over the next weeks the message changed very little, for despite the efforts of the Lighthouse Service no trace was ever found of the *Mignonette* or any of its men.

The Treasury Department sent a revenue cutter to search the waters around Brazos Santiago, while lighthouse keepers all up the coast were alerted to watch the shorelines for any fragments of the vessel or remains of its complement of men. The keeper of the Point Isabel Lighthouse even rented a horse so that he could ride the beaches in search, but nothing, nothing was ever found. The Gulf of Mexico simply opened up and swallowed the *Mignonette* and its men.

In October 1887 Lighthouse Engineer Heuer sent to Washington a formal report on the loss of the ship, summarizing the futile efforts that had been made to locate any fragments of the vessel or remains of the men, concluding, "All on board are lost."

Heuer asked his superiors, "As all of these men signed pay rolls for the month of September, I have to request to be authorized to pay their widows or next of kin the amount for the month of September or for as much of that month as the Board may feel warranted in authorizing." Watching its pennies, the Lighthouse Board decided that the heirs were due just three week's pay because the sixteen men had left the service of the government on September 21—the day the *Mignonette* had gone over the sandbar at Brazos Santiago Pass and into the gulf never to be seen again.

Hot Tamale Vendors

For decades hot tamale vendors in summer and winter have been part of the Texas scene. Their Mexican specialty food consists of minced meat and peppers rolled in cornmeal and wrapped in corn shucks to be steamed till done.

Writing about Brownsville in 1893, Lieutenant W. H. Chatfield in *The Twin Cities of the Border* reported that tamales in the border country were a universal food among the Hispanic part of the population, while "there are many Americans who relish them fully as much as do the natives." He noted that in Brownsville the vendors were principally women, who worked all day to prepare their fare and then sell it in the evenings on the market square.

"Americans select the vendor who sells the smallest and the hottest tamales," the observer remarked, noting that tamales sold for 12½ cents a dozen. After buying them, the customers "then . . . hasten home, occasionally shifting the steaming hot 'brown paper parcel' from one hand to the other."

Eating tamales, the lieutenant explained, was a simple process: "When the corn shuck in which the tamales are steamed is removed, a roll of corn meal is disclosed and it is eaten like a banana." Describing the dish, he wrote, "there is a streak of finely minced chicken or beef in the center, highly seasoned with red pepper, of course."

Half a century ago, Early Caldwell of Athens, Texas, claimed to be "The World's Greatest Tamale King." Starting in November 1920, the Black man prepared tamales in his home three times a week, selling them on the courthouse square in Athens on what was called "Early's Corner." Each year he printed up advertising calendars bearing his likeness, and he gave them to his friends and customers. Today these calendars are collectors' items.

The paper wrappers in which tamales were sold proved to be useful to a vendor in Nacogdoches back in the days of prohibition. He called out as he pushed his cart through the streets of the town, "Hot Tamales! Hot Tamales! And that ain't all!"—the last phrase delivered in insinuating tones. Not only were his hot tamales paper wrapped, but inside his cart were additional newspaper-wrapped packages, some of them containing corn whiskey of the peddler's own production.

The most prominent of the Nacogdoches tamale vendors of the 1950s was Will Risper, a white-mustached Black man in his seventies. Vending from a horse-drawn cart that looked more like a milk wagon, he sold not only tamales but also hamburgers, hot dogs, sodas, and candy. Risper had a special way to keep his food hot several hours into the day although he had no stove on the wagon. He placed rocks, which he had heated all night in his wood-burning range at home, into the metal boxes in which he kept food.

For eight years, Risper drew his wagon with a handsome gelding called Old Coley. The horse, according to the tamale man, didn't need any driving. "He knew my run and he would stop and go on traffic lights." The horse was a tremendous asset for Risper, who was hard of hearing. If one of his customers called out to him, Old Coley would stop. The vender declared, "He was a horse with heart and soul."

The Mysterious Death of T. J. Chambers

The pretty, white, two-story house called "Chambersea" where Thomas Jefferson Chambers used to live still stands as a historical landmark in Anahuac, but to this day no one knows why the Texas hero was killed there in 1865.

A native of Virginia, Chambers had lived in Kentucky before immigrating from the United States to Mexico city at the age of twenty-four in 1826. Already by this time he had studied law and had been admitted to the bar in both Kentucky and Alabama.

With his legal training completed in the United States, Chambers next devoted his efforts to learning the Spanish language and to mastering the Mexican legal system. After the Virginian had spent three years in Mexico, Vice Governor Victor Blanco of the State of Coahuila and Texas appointed him surveyor general of the state. (At this time Coahuila and Texas were joined as a single state in the Mexican republic.)

Chambers first worked as a land surveyor for the Mexican government west of the Rio Grande, but in late 1929 he moved to present-day East Texas, making his headquarters in Nacogdoches. There he became acquainted with English-speaking settlers who for the past decade had been moving to Texas from the United States.

February 1834 saw the promotion of Chambers to the office of state attorney for the State of Coahuila and Texas. Later that year he assumed the role of judge in a superior court which had been established for Texas. For his services to the Mexican government, Chambers received payment of thirty leagues of land, which today would amount to about 137,000 acres.

Though he had been serving as a judge for the Mexican government, Chambers's sentiments lay with the Anglo-American settlers when the Texas Revolution broke out against Mexico in late 1835. Once Texas declared its independence, he offered his extensive lands as collateral for the new government in raising money to pay for its war against Mexico.

The provisional government of Texas commissioned Chambers a major general and sent him to the United States to recruit men, arms, and money for the revolution. There he was more than successful, dispatching 1,915 volunteers to fight in Texas and spending $23,621 for guns, munitions, and supplies.

Following the Texas Revolution, Chambers devoted much of his life to legally defending the titles to his lands granted by the Mexican government, some of which encompassed the site of Austin, the new capital for the Republic of Texas.

Always keen for political activity, Chambers became an ardent supporter of Texas secession before the Civil War. After participating in the Texas secession convention, he ran unsuccessfully for Texas governor in 1863. Chambers traveled to Virginia to offer his services to the Confederate Army, where he fought in a number of engagements. He was injured in battle and was back home at Anahuac by spring 1865.

T. J. Chambers was sitting in a rocking chair in his white frame home with his two daughters and wife a little before bedtime on the evening of March 15, 1865. The Civil War would last for another month, but things were quiet at Anahuac.

The stillness of the evening was broken by a flash of light and crack of explosion when through an outside window an unknown assassin shot the Texas statesman in the chest. Chambers's wife, Abbe, ran to him, but his life ran away as the blood ran from his wound. That night he died in the little, white, two-story house with five-pointed Texas stars in the gables.

To this day the identity of the murderer is unknown, though historians have speculated that he may have been a vengeful Unionist or a disgruntled adversary from one of the many land title suits. Perhaps the greatest mystery, however, involves the painted portrait of Chambers that hung in the same room—where the chest also was penetrated by a bullet.

Old-time Texas Dance Parties

In springtime 1987 the city council of Anson, Texas, repealed a fifty-year-old ordinance prohibiting dancing so that the high school senior class could hold a prom, but dancing has been a popular activity for Texans for well over a century and a half.

Dilue Rose Harris, who came to Texas as a girl in April 1833, filled her diary with references to toe-tapping evenings on the dance floor. Her first dancing experience, in fact, was in Texas.

In April 1834 she wrote, "One evening Mrs. Dyer sent her brother, Harvey Stafford, to invite mother to attend a dancing party at her house," adding, "We children were delighted." They went the two miles to the Dyer home, arriving there before dark. "The people soon began to arrive, among them several young ladies."

"As soon as the house was lighted," Harris remembered, "a Negro man came in with a fiddle and commenced playing." The teenagers began dancing, and "one of the boys asked me to dance." She had to decline, for "I had never danced."

That evening, however, Dilue Harris looked on and watched the different steps until she felt that she could replicate them. Then, she related, "Harvey Stafford asked me to be his partner in an old Virginia reel. I went on the floor and danced till morning." July 1834 brought an occasion when the Americans in Mexican Texas celebrated the United States Independence Day as their own holiday.

Together with a barbecue and a quilting bee, they marked the occasion with a dance. "It was a grand affair for the times," Harris said. "The young people thought it was magnificent." Music for the event was provided by three Black men who alternated playing on a fiddle. "One Negro man got an iron pin and clevis, used at the end of a cart tongue or plough beam, and beat time with the fiddle." The third beat a tin pan.

The Fourth of July dance lasted from three o'clock in the afternoon until dawn the next morning. "Everybody went home in a good humor, none more so than the Negro musicians," as they were paid for playing the fiddles and beating the "clevis and tin pan," wrote Harris.

On yet another occasion, this time in April 1835, Harris attended a dance that had been organized so that the local young men could meet the pretty daughter in an English family who had just immigrated to Texas. As before, happy feet pattered across the floor of a log cabin home all through the evening.

"When daylight came," Harris fondly remembered, "all went home wishing the night had been six months long."

2½ Percent Commission on All Slaves Sold

When you visit Galveston, Texas, you can go to see the home of one of the builders of the city—John S. Sydnor. The restored Greek Revival house named "Powhatan" is preserved by the Galveston Garden Club at 3427 Avenue O and is open to the public. When you go there, however, you probably won't learn everything about original owner John S. Sydnor.

"Negroes Wanted in Galveston" read the bold print in a full-page advertisement for John S. Sydnor's auction house in the 1861 *Texas Almanac*. Although there never was an especially active commerce in slaves at Galveston because of the lack of nearby agricultural land and the illegality of the overseas slave trade, the antebellum economy of the city still required that the ownership of enslaved Africans change from time to time, and a demand existed for a slave market. Sydnor supplied that demand.

Having been born near Richmond, Virginia, in 1812, John S. Sydnor came first to Texas in 1838, settling permanently at Galveston the next year. Economic times were hard in Texas, and Sydnor rightly judged that he could make money in the produce business. Accordingly he established a large market garden and dairy, for which he issued printed paper "checks" worth certain values in produce. At a time when Texas money was nearly worthless, his "checks" circulated in Galveston as small change redeemable in milk and vegetables.

In 1843 Sydnor entered the commission business, and in this way he became part of the slave trade. For each slave sold in his auction house on the Strand in Galveston, he received a percentage commission for each dollar of purchase price.

While Sydnor was building his slave auction business, he also was becoming prominent in local politics. In 1846 a majority of the Galveston voters elected Sydnor mayor of the city. Through his efforts as mayor, the Texas legislature passed a law allowing the Board of Aldermen of Galveston to levy and collect a special tax for the support of public schools within the corporate limits of the town.

Within a short time, the city government was able to rent a large building and hire a corps of male and female teachers to open the school to the children of white families. The response in numbers of pupils was almost overwhelming, but later municipal administrations failed to continue support and the first free schools in Galveston were closed. Even so, John S. Sydnor is recognized as the founder of public education in Galveston.

Remaining in the Crescent City after his mayoral term, Sydnor became even more active in the Galveston slave trade. In 1860 he advertised, for instance, "The number of Negroes consigned to me for sale has induced me to give the business more particular attention." He reduced his commission to only 2½ percent, while he made arrangements for slaves awaiting sale to be employed temporarily in a warehouse adjacent to his auction house in order to reduce expenses for their owners.

Now, when you walk through the palatial "Powhatan" house that John S. Sydnor built in Galveston, look down at the beautiful 5½ inch center-matched pine floors and consider how many human beings that John S. Sydnor had to sell on the block at 2½ percent commission in order to pay for those boards.

The First Juneteenth

In early June 1865, Confederate major H. A. Wallace heard that Southern troops in Houston had laid down their arms in surrender. He boarded the boat, *Island City*, and went to find out if indeed the Civil War had ended.

Learning that indeed the Union had defeated the South and realizing that neither federal nor Confederate authorities were in control of affairs, he commandeered the *Island City* as his own and proceeded to use it to establish a waterborne freight business between Houston and Galveston.

When Wallace arrived in Galveston on Sunday, June 17, 1865, from a distance he could see black men on the wharf throwing their hats into the air. When he approached close enough, he called out to them, "What's the matter?" One replied, "We's free now."

"What makes you free?" he yelled out to one of the former slaves. "Yankees come down on ships on the outside to free us," the joyous man answered.

Two days later, on June 19, federal general Gordon Granger arrived in Galveston formally to take charge of Texas, although federal troops had preceded him in the city by two weeks. On this day, Juneteenth as it is now known, Granger made official the emancipation of the slaves in Texas.

According to Granger's "General Orders No. 3" issued on June 19, "The people are informed that, in accordance with a proclamation from the Executive of the United States, all slaves are free." The enunciation also stated that "this involves an absolute equality of personal rights and property between former masters and slaves and the connection theretofore existing between them becomes that between employer and hired labor."

Granger's announcement additionally advised the freedmen to remain at their homes and to work for wages. Galveston, however, soon became a magnet for freed slaves from the hinterland of Texas, and hundreds soon began gathering in the port city.

The real day of celebration for the former bondsmen in Galveston wasn't June 19, but rather Sunday, June 17, when Major Wallace saw the men tossing their hats into the air on the Galveston wharf. *The Galveston Tri-Weekly News* reported, "Last Sunday the people of Galveston were astonished at the number of colored individuals of all shades congregated here. The like had not been seen since the war began." Condescendingly, the paper commented, "The dress, airs and swagger of this motley multitude would have done credit to the shoddy aristocracy of the North."

Many of the newly freed slaves, however, were interested in far more than merely celebrating their newly found freedom. They sought to become their own masters. "There seems to be a very general ambition among the Negro women of the city to go to housekeeping for themselves," reported the *Galveston Weekly News* on June 28. "Some of them have rented very genteel cottages at a rent fully twice as high as before the war," the paper noted. At first it seemed surprising that the former slaves would have the money to rent such houses, but then it became apparent that some of them had scrupulously saved money that they had accumulated over the years, some of them having more cash on hand than their bankrupt former owners.

Bemoaning the loss of the slaves, the *Weekly News* concluded in self-pity, "Some of our wealthiest and most respectable citizens have not a servant left, and . . . ladies are now to do their own cooking and housework."

A Cargo of Ostriches

Sailing ships were commonplace in Galveston a century ago, but ostriches on the streets were not. Thus the arrival on January 25, 1887, of a cargo of forty-four South African ostriches on the Swedish bark *Krona* created quite a stir.

Wanting to provide a report to curious residents of the city, a journalist from the *Galveston Daily News* managed to hitch a ride on the yawl with Customs Inspector Delaney when he sailed out to the *Krona* to inspect its avian cargo. Delany's duty as a customs officer was to examine the cargoes of all foreign vessels entering the port.

The reporter and the customs inspector, on arrival at the *Krona*, learned that two Americans named Cawston and Hoyle had chartered the ship to carry the giant flightless birds from Natal in South Africa to Galveston. From the Texas port, they planned to transport the birds by railway to Los Angeles, California, where they were starting an ostrich ranch. Galveston was just a layover on their journey halfway around the world.

Today one might wonder why the two Americans would want an ostrich ranch in the first place. The answer can be found in high fashion. Ostrich plumes in fans and other clothing accessories were highly sought after by fashion-conscious ladies in the 1880s, and ostrich raising soon became a fad in sunny Southern California, where the climate was similar to that of ostrich-raising country in South Africa.

Cawston and Hoyle explained to the reporter that finding the ostriches had not been an easy chore. "We bought them at Natal, and had to travel all over the country to get them," they said. The men bought their ostriches in Natal rather than in the Cape Colony, where the birds were much more common, to avoid the latter region's heavy export tax.

The two American buyers had taken great pains preparing the inside of the sailing ship for the huge birds. "The birds are arranged in stalls as near the center of the hold as possible," the newspaperman reported. "Each stall contains one [ostrich], and between the rows of stalls are apartments, or paddocks, into which the birds are turned every day for exercise." To protect the animals during rough seas, the insides of the wooden stalls were padded.

Rations for just under fifty ostriches required logistical planning. "For food for the birds," the buyers told the reporter, "we started with two thousand cabbages, thirty-five sacks of sweet potatoes, one-half ton of bran, one ton of crushed bones and many bushels of carrots and turnips." Even this was insufficient for the whole trip, and they stopped at the islands of St. Helena and Barbados to take on fresh water and additional feedstuffs, including half a ton of prickly pears at St. Helena.

Health represented a major concern for the bird importers. They regularly cleaned the stalls and paddocks, removing waste and keeping fresh sand in the bottoms of the cages. "We have done our best to keep things clean and sweet down below," one of them declared.

Locals in Galveston had their chance to view the birds the same day that the printed report appeared in the *Galveston News*. On January 26, 1887, the ostriches were unloaded at the brick wharf "in order to rest" before they could continue westward by rail for their new home in California and things could return to normal on the streets of Galveston.

How I Captured Santa Anna

Georgia native Joel W. Robison was one of the nine hundred revolutionaries who participated in the defeat of the Mexican army at San Jacinto on April 21, 1836, which won Texas independence. The next day, however, he was a member of an even more select group. He and five other men unknowingly captured the escaping Mexican general, Antonio Lopez de Santa Anna.

"I was one of a detachment of 30 or 40 men commanded by Colonel [Edward] Burleson, which left . . . on the morning after the battle to pursue the fugitive enemy," Robison related. Departing camp, the Texans headed toward Vince's Bayou, knowing that straggling Mexican troops might be trapped there since the bridge over the bayou had been burned.

The party succeeded in picking up three or four Mexican soldiers. Colonel Burleson gave each of them notes penciled on scraps of paper in English stating that they had surrendered and directing them to proceed on foot to the Texan camp to join the other prisoners. There was nowhere for the defeated men to escape, being so far from home in Mexico, and the notes were for their own protection from other Texan troops.

Finally tiring of the meager results from their search for stragglers, the Texans broke up into smaller groups. Robison was one of the six men in his party.

About two miles east of Vince's Bayou, the six men came to a ravine that led toward Buffalo Bayou with several groves of trees scattered along its length. As they rode along on horseback, "we discovered a man standing in the prairie near one of the groves." Robison remembered that the man was a Mexican dressed in civilian clothing consisting of a blue hat, a waistcoat, and a pair of trousers, and carrying a rude bundle.

"I was the only member of our party who spoke any Spanish," Robison related, so he volunteered to interrogate the man. "In reply to the question whether he knew where [Generals] Santa Anna and Cos were, he said he presumed they had gone to the Brazos," Robison reported.

One of the Texans, Edward Miles, first placed the prisoner on his horse and walked about a mile back to the road. "Here he ordered the prisoner to dismount, which he did with great reluctance," Robison reported, adding "he walked slowly and apparently with pain." The captive explained that he was a cavalryman and unaccustomed to walking.

Miles, who Robison remembered as "a rough, reckless fellow," had picked up a Mexican lance on the battlefield that morning. "With the weapon he occasionally slightly pricked the prisoner to accelerate his pace—which sometimes amounted to a trot," Robison said. After a while Miles tired of his cat-and-mouse game with the hapless prisoner. The six Texans debated what to do with the footsore Mexican, some proposing that they simply allow him to proceed to the Texan camp on his own. Miles, on the other hand, insisted that the captive be left behind and that then "he would kill him."

"Finally my compassion for the prisoner moved me to mount him behind me," Robison related. "I also took charge of his bundle."

As they returned to the Texan camp, Robison and the prisoner conversed in Spanish. "Did General Houston command in person in the action yesterday?" the captive wanted to know. He could hardly believe Robison when the Texan said that only nine hundred Texans had been in the fight. "I remember asking him why he came to Texas to fight against us, to which he replied that he was a private soldier, and was bound to obey his officers," Robison later reported. "I asked him if he had a family," Robison said. "He replied in the affirmative, and when I inquired, Do you expect to see them again? his only answer was a shrug of the shoulders."

When the six Texans with their one prisoner rode into the camp where the other surrendered Mexican troops were being detained, "What was our astonishment, as we approached the guard, to hear the prisoners exclaiming 'El Presidente! El Presidente!'" Only then did Robison and his compatriots realize that they inadvertently had captured Mexican general Lopez de Santa Anna himself. Immediately armed soldiers conducted the new captive to the presence of Texan commander Sam Houston, where the general formally surrendered.

Robison remained in possession of Santa Anna's bundle, and afterward out of curiosity he opened it to see what was inside. There he found an inferior quality blanket, a white linen sheet, a grey vest with gold buttons, and a gourd canteen for water.

Later Robison called on Santa Anna while in camp and offered to return the bundle and its contents. "He declined receiving it, and expressed himself very grateful for the kindness I had shown him."

Indeed, Robison's compassion had saved the life of "the Napoleon of the West."

Almost Killed at San Jacinto

Corning to Texas to fight in its rebellion against Mexico, Alphonso Steele almost lost his life to the bayonet of one of his fellow rebels.

In November 1835 the Kentucky native joined a company of American insurgents that had been raised in Louisiana. When the men reached Texas, however, they found that independence had not been declared and that there was no formally organized army for them to join. The company disbanded and its members went their own ways.

Steele ended up working temporarily in a hotel at Washington-on-the-Brazos, Texas, where later elected representatives from the various parts of Texas met and on March 2, 1836, formally declared independence from Mexico. Employed at the hotel where some of the delegates stayed, "I ground corn on a steel mill to make bread for the men who signed the declaration of independence," he said.

About this time Steele joined a group of men who were headed to join the Texans gathered at the Alamo, but when they reached the Colorado River they learned of the fall of that garrison. "He then moved down the river and fell in with General [Sam] Houston close to Beeson's Crossing, on the Colorado." In this way Steele found himself at San Jacinto at the time of the battle on April 21, 1836, in which Texas won its independence from Mexico. His role in the fight was one of a common soldier, and he ended up being one of the thirty-four Texans who were wounded.

As part of the left wing of the Texan forces under Sidney Sherman, Steele was in the group of men who attacked a light breastworks of baggage that the Mexican troops had put up as an outer perimeter of their camp. "We were ordered to move forward and hold our fire until word was given to shoot," he recalled later in life. When they got to within fifty to sixty yards of the Mexicans, the insurrectionists finally were given the order to fire. Steele remembered, "We were ordered to fire and all discipline, as far as Sherman's regiment was concerned, was at an end."

Steele reported that the Texans were firing their guns as rapidly as possible into the Mexican ranks. "As soon as we fired, every man went to reloading his gun, and he who first got his gun ready moved on, not waiting for orders." The former rebel continued, "I got my gun loaded and rushed into the timber and fired again. When the second volley was poured into them, they broke and ran."

Having reloaded again, Steele followed the retreating Mexican soldiers. "I . . . ran a little ahead of our men and threw up my gun to shoot, when I was shot down." Dave Rusk, one of Steele's compatriots, was nearby, and when Steele went down he asked several of the men to stay with him, to which Steele protested, "No, take them on."

As he lay on the ground, another Texan insurgent asked Steele if he could take his pistol, but, as Steele remembered, "I was bleeding so at the nose and mouth that I couldn't speak." The man then realized the situation and just stooped down and took the gun on into battle.

After the close of the eighteen-minute fight, one of the Texans brought a horse over to Steele in order to carry him to medical attention. For reasons unknown, the man sat Steele down amid a group of dead Mexican soldiers, but, as he later recalled, "I was so blind I could see nothing and I sat down on a dead Mexican."

While Steele, temporarily blinded by his own blood, sat among the corpses, some other Texans came along "sticking . . . [Mexicans] wounded with their bayonets." Thinking Steele was an injured Mexican, they were about to put him out of his misery when Texan Tom Green chanced along and stopped them.

Concluding his tale of San Jacinto, Steele reported, "Then I was put on a horse and started to our camp."

Steele survived his wounds, becoming a farmer and stock raiser, first near Montgomery, and later in Limestone County, where he died at the home of a grandson in 1911, honored as a veteran of San Jacinto.

1838 Murder and Execution in Houston

Texan cities like Houston have reputations today for violence, but the brutality goes back to the beginnings of urban life in Texas.

Houston was no more than a few months old when young Kentucky lawyer John Hunter Herndon arrived there in January 1838. On the 23rd of the month, he penned in his diary that he had arrived at three o'clock in the afternoon and already had "formed a bad opinion of the place, which time will correct or confirm." As he stayed there for the next months, the twenty-five year old found much that he liked and much that he disliked.

The roughness and cheapness of life in Houston appalled the well-to-do young man, who nevertheless remained there and, despite the rowdyism, began practicing law. Herndon managed to while away his free time in the Bayou City by playing whist and billiards, drinking moderately, hunting wildfowl, and visiting with young ladies. Sometimes he even confided in his diary about going to church just because certain young ladies might be found there.

As an attorney, the Kentuckian took more than a passing interest in local legal affairs and current trials in the city, noting in his journal entry for Friday, March 23, the conviction of John C. C. Quick for murder. Three months earlier Quick had stabbed to death one W. M. Brigham with a dirk at a gaming table in the Houston House, a local watering hole and gaming den.

The local newspaper, the *Telegraph and Texas Register*, reported, "Several persons who recognized him state that he has committed five murders." The paper continued to predict that Quick could well swing from the gallows, noting that a "halter" might before long cause him to have "more elevated notions of our fellow citizens." Held in jail for three months, Quick went to trial in March 1838, and he was convicted of murder on the 23rd. Herndon recorded in his journal that Quick, who he characterized as a "malicious looking devil," did not change "a feature or muscle of his face upon the verdict being announced."

Justice was not slow in frontier Houston. Five days later a wagon driven under a guard of a hundred militia members carried Quick and another convicted killer named Read to the city execution grounds, described by the press as "a beautiful islet of timber, situated in the prairie about a mile south of the city."

As was the custom of the day, a large crowd of spectators attended the hanging; Herndon estimated over two thousand people. "Among the whole," he noted, "not a sympathetic tear was dropped." Despite the callous attitude of the onlookers, however, the murderer proceeded with his speech. According to the young attorney, "Quick addressed the crowd in a stern, composed and hardened manner," the press noting that he "expiated upon the dangerous influence of gambling and the practice of wearing concealed weapons."

The paper reported, "He met his fate with great firmness," which Herndon confirmed by writing, he was "unmoved up to the moment of swinging off the cart." The editor of the *Telegraph and Texas Register* concluded that the two murderers had "atoned for their faults" with the most terrible of the earthly punishments and by praying that they might "find favor at that mysterious tribunal whose decisions are for eternity."

Lubbock's Buckskin Britches

Francis R. Lubbock, best known to history as governor of Texas during the Civil War, had anything but good words to share on the topic of buckskin clothing. As a participant on an expedition against hostile Indians in 1838, he wore a new pair of buckskin trousers that gave him constant discomfort.

Lubbock had been born in South Carolina in 1815, and he came to Texas shortly after its war for independence in 1836. Settling first at Velasco and soon moving to Houston, he claimed to have been one of the first merchants at the Bayou City. Lubbock served as a clerk for the House of Representatives of the Second Texas Congress, and then in 1838 President Sam Houston appointed him comptroller for the Republic of Texas.

In November 1838 Lubbock received a temporary release from his civilian duties to join a party of Houstonians who were assembling to pursue a band of Indians that had been raiding the settlements along the Brazos River near its falls, not far from present-day Marlin.

Lubbock in his autobiography stated that the warriors had become so troublesome that "the government determined to put a battalion in the field to chastise them." Major George W. Bonnell, for whom Mount Bonnell near Austin later was named, commanded the expedition.

Before leaving with the party, Lubbock had new clothes sewn especially for use on the expedition. "I had made for me a pair of fine buckskin pants such as worn by frontiersmen," he noted. Buckskin, as young Lubbock discovered, was not a very practical material for field use. It proved to be oppressively hot during warm weather and quite cold and slow to dry when the weather turned chilly and rainy.

"We left Houston in a very wet and cold time, and in a few nights afterwards we encountered a dreadful and disastrous sleet," he later wrote. "We were without tents and suffered fearfully."

While away from the main party scouting for Indians in a small group of men, Lubbock and his companions were overtaken one night by a heavy thunderstorm. "I was lying in a low place, so that the water ran against me in a flood, saturating my buckskins."

Not thinking about any possible consequences, he backed up to a hot mesquite fire to dry himself out. Before Lubbock realized what was happening, he discovered "my pants had crawled up to my knees." For the next few days he had to ride in the skintight britches, unable to remove them since they were the only pants he had.

As time passed, the buckskins failed to release their grip on Lubbock's legs. Instead, "they got tighter and tighter all the time until we reached the main camp."

After he finally rejoined the larger party, "I had in a manner to cut them off my limbs."Concluding the story of his shrink-to-fit britches, Lubbock pronounced, "I have never owned a pair of buckskin pants since. They are more entertaining in a picture or a romance than they are on one's own shanks."

Dog Days of Summer

"The dog days are at hand, and curs and puppies are beginning to exhibit the usual symptoms of irritability," reported the editor of the *Telegraph and Texas Register* at Houston on August 10, 1842. "We may therefore expect that dog fights will be for a season quite frequent," he added.

I had heard about the "dog days of summer" all my life, but I really didn't know what they actually were. Then my friend, Don Garland, a filmmaker who used to run the planetarium at the Fort Worth Museum of Science and History, set me straight.

The dog days of summer, according to Don, took their name from the star Sirius, "the dog star," which generally becomes visible during August in the early morning sky.

The brightest star in the heavens, second only to our own sun, Sirius is visible just above the horizon early in the morning during August. Its brilliance comes from its comparative nearness to earth, only fifty-one million miles away. "Sirius is a bright, shining star just above the southeastern horizon at dawn," Don told me. "Depending on atmospheric conditions, it can sparkle and appear to change color and dance around."

Sirius forms part of the constellation of stars known as *Canis Major*, "large dog," which the ancient Greeks envisioned as being one of the hounds belonging to the celestial hunter, Orion. Thus it came to be known as the "dog star."

The myths about Sirius go back even farther to include the Egyptians. Garland explained, "When the ancient Egyptians saw Sirius, they knew that the Nile was about to flood. They didn't know that rains were happening in the interior of Africa—they associated the annual flooding with the rising of Sirius."

Back in Texas in 1842, the editor of the *Telegraph and Texas Register* wished in print that the cantankerous effects of Sirius on the canine population would not spread to the humans in Houston. "We shall be happy if loafers and biped puppies do not catch the contagion and disturb the usual quiet of our improving city with brawls and riots," he declared. "We hope," he wrote, "neither the malign influence of the dog star nor any other cause will break the charm and let loose the angry passions to renew the scenes of discord and wrangling that disgraced our fair city in its early days."

Slavery in the Classifieds

Black slavery in Texas before the Civil War left its traces many places where you might not expect them. One of these places where I stumbled onto the "peculiar institution" was in the classified ads printed in the old Houston *Telegraph and Texas Register* newspaper in the 1850s.

The first mention of enslaved Africans that I noticed in the classifieds was wedged between advertisements for Sam Lathrop's Circus and for plows and wagons sold by A. S. Ruthven. There, on page 3 of the January 2, 1852, paper, Henry Sampson advertised for "sale two Negroes, man and wife." He described the two as "capable servants accustomed to farm work," adding that "both will be sold for the very low price of $700, if applied for immediately."

The irony of seeing human beings advertised for sale along with farm equipment and circus tickets did more than catch my attention; I started looking out for more such notices.

About the end of 1852, on Friday, December 10, at the top of page 3 in the *Telegraph and Texas Register*, an ad for an entire family appeared above an advertisement for Martin & Butt, dealer in stoves and tinware. "For Sale, a family of Plantation Negroes," the notice began. I pondered about the composition of the family and read further to answer my own question. The slave family consisted of, as the ad read, "a man 28 years old, woman 26 years old, two boys, one 4 and the other 2 ½ years old." Since I found no record of how the sale was consummated, I never was able to determine whether the Black family managed to stay together or was separated in its sale.

One slave appeared at least twice in the *Telegraph and Texas Register* classifieds. He was Harrison, a slave belonging to William W. McMahan, owner of a plantation on Oyster Creek in Fort Bend County. "Ran away from the plantation," began the ad from August 27, 1852. McMahan advertised a cash reward for anyone who could capture and return Harrison.

According to McMahan, the slave escaped on August 19, while delivering clothing from Houston to the Oyster Creek plantation. "Harrison carried off with him an old brown horse, saddle, bridle, and saddle-bags," the bags containing the said garments. McMahan noted, "Harrison will in all probability try to pass himself off as a free man under an assumed name, as he has done before."

Some slave catcher apparently nabbed Harrison and returned him to McMahan because later in 1852, on December 3, the slaveholder placed another ad in the *Telegraph and Texas Register*. This time he again offered a reward for the return of Harrison, who had run away anew "about the 20th of October last."

Harrison was becoming a persistent "runaway," which certainly would not have endeared him to McMahan. The planter this time gave the following description of his repeatedly escaped property: "Harrison [is] aged about 30, of dark complexion, about five feet high," adding that the slave had "a crippling walk, from a hurt which he received some years ago."

McMahan noted that Harrison had escaped on foot from his Oyster Creek plantation, "but it is believed he stole an iron grey mare from the neighbor hood." We don't know when or whether Harrison was captured this time. In fact, we wouldn't know about his escape at all were it not for McMahan's classified advertisement between notices for J. W. Benedict Boot & Shoe Store and W. Henry Eliot's "fresh drugs and medicines just received from New York and Philadelphia." Traces of the Texas Black past certainly may be found in the classifieds.

O'Henry and the Swedish Poet

"It was a case of mistaken identity . . ." is how John P. Sjolander began his remembrance of inviting the unknown O'Henry on a visit to his home at Cedar Bayou near Houston. O'Henry, whose real name was William Sidney Porter, was at the time the unsuccessful editor of a failed humor magazine, and he was out of work. In a few years, however, he would become one of the most famous of all American short story writers.

Sjolander and Porter met in 1895 on the docks at Houston, where Sjolander (pronounced Shol-ander) was delivering watermelons by boat for the local produce market. An immigrant to Texas from Sweden, Sjolander already had become recognized as a gifted poet and was known as "the sage of Cedar Bayou." He still is remembered as one of the finest of all Texas poets.

"While unloading melons from the boat onto wagons, . . . I noticed a man standing on the bank of the bayou watching," Sjolander later wrote.

When the wagons were loaded, the Swede turned around to where the man had been standing only to see his back as he began walking away. From behind, the man looked as if he might be Sjolander's friend, William Cowper Brann, editor of the *Iconoclast* magazine in Austin.

"Hello, Brann; where are you going?" Sjolander called out. "The man turned, smiling, and faced me, and then I saw he was not the Great Iconoclast. Still, there was a resemblance," he said.

The stranger then walked over toward Sjolander, who invited him under the shade of an awning on the boat so they could talk. It turned out that the man was a North Carolinian named Sidney Porter who had purchased the *Iconoclast* from Brann and who had overhauled it into a humor magazine called *The Rolling Stone*. The venture had failed, however, and Porter had come to Houston looking for work as a stonecutter. The Swede joshed him for seeking that type of employment in Houston "where there was not a stone to be found large enough to throw at a stray dog."

Having nothing better to do with himself, Porter accompanied Sjolander on his boat the next day to Cedar Bayou, and there he stayed as the poet's guest for the next two weeks.

One day while visiting at Cedar Bayou, Porter came across a small book giving the names and addresses of magazines and newspapers that at the time were seeking manuscripts for "literary wares." When Sjolander saw him copying down information from its pages, he later recalled, "I told him he need not do so, for he could have the book, as I had no use for it." By this time, Sjolander's poetry had become so popular that publishers were coming to him asking for it.

"During the time he was with me on the boat and at my home," Sjolander related, "I sent a couple of stories to a newspaper in New Orleans, from which I had acceptance before he left, and I remember he asked me why I did not follow story writing altogether."

"Try it yourself," Sjolander answered, not thinking any more of the suggestion. "I may," Porter answered, but that was all he said.

The two men parted near Houston at the end of the two weeks, and Sjolander never saw Porter again. "Some years later I had a short note from him dated somewhere in Pennsylvania," the poet noted. "But it was sometime after that before I learned that the Sidney Porter I had known had become the well-known short story writer, O'Henry."

Under Fire at Sabine Pass

The 1863 Battle of Sabine Pass, in which forty-seven Confederate artillerymen drove off an invading force of six Union gunboats and over five thousand federal troops, is legendary in Texas Civil War history. The story of the fight, however, is almost always told from the perspective of the rebel defenders.

Fortunately a number of the Union men involved in the engagement left their own accounts of the fight, and they are just as exciting as those told by the rebels. One of the remembrances comes from Lieutenant Henry C. Dane, who was a signal officer on the Union gunboat *Sachem*.

The federal strategy in attacking Sabine Pass was to capture a supposed weakly defended point at the mouth of the Sabine River on the Gulf of Mexico. From that point, the invading troops could proceed up the railroad to Beaumont, which would be a perfect base of operations for assaulting Houston, eighty-five miles away to the west on the railway down the level coastal plain.

Union officers assembled a flotilla of vessels consisting of six gunboats and seventeen troop transports loaded with several thousand men and five artillery batteries to establish a beachhead at Sabine Pass. They arrived from New Orleans at the mouth of the Sabine on September 7, 1863. The officers held a council of war, and final plans were made to assault an earthen fort held by rebels on the Texas side of the river just above its mouth.

Known as Fort Griffin, the fortification had been built a month earlier and was armed with just six pieces of artillery. Forty-seven men defended the post under the immediate command of Richard W. Dowling, a red-headed, blue-eyed Irish immigrant in his twenties. During the previous couple of weeks, the Confederates had been practicing the aim of their cannons at wooden stobs driven into the mud of the Sabine River about where they expected possible enemy vessels might approach, so they were prepared when the flotilla assembled at sea outside the mouth of the river.

The initial assault force consisted of the gunboats *Clifton* and *Sachem*, the latter carrying Lieutenant Dane. They were to divert the guns of Fort Griffin from transports that were to land men on the Texas bank of the river, but things didn't progress that far.

About four o'clock on the afternoon of September 8, the two gunboats started steaming up the Sabine. "The *Sachem* was moving up the Louisiana channel with all her guns talking," Lieutenant Dane recalled, "while the *Clifton* took the Texas channel, which ran close under the fort." Not a shot came from the nondescript earthen fort, where the gunners waited behind cover until the Yankees got within range of their guns.

Lieutenant Dane called the attention of the captain of the *Sachem* to the wooden stobs stuck in the side of the river ahead of the gunboat, who replied gruffly, "Well, what of them?" When the vessel reached that point, everyone on board realized that they were range markers for the rebel artillery, but by then it was too late.

"The moment we passed the first pole a flash of flame shot from the parapet, a white cloud rose over it and 'wh-i-ng' went a shell fifty feet above our heads," Dane said. Three more shells overshot the *Sachem*, but the fifth made its mark. "Before I could restore myself to a full perpendicular, 'Wh-o-o-ing! chuck!' came the fifth, passing through us from side to side, enveloping me in a cloud of splinters." Catching shots from all six Southern guns, the *Sachem* soon became pulverized. "Our railings were vanishing, our decks were plowed and torn and our men were falling in squads," Dane recalled.

Once the *Sachem* was grounded in the mud, the Confederate artillerymen turned their attention to the *Clifton*, which had approached to within about five hundred yards. Dane reported, "In a few minutes a white cloud rose from the *Clifton*'s deck and a minute later a white flag was flying." It had surrendered.

Meanwhile the Yankee gunners on the *Sachem* kept on firing the two usable artillery pieces, but that could not last much longer. Dane related, "'Wh-i-ng! crack! chink!' came a shot through our side, through the boiler and away into the mud." The cannonball released boiling hot water and steam to spew onto the deck of the vessel, horribly burning many of the men who had survived the fight that far.

"I don't know whether to surrender or not," exclaimed the captain, but as soon as he turned toward the sea he realized that others had already made the decision for him. The entire Union flotilla had turned and was sailing back to New Orleans, defeated by Dick Dowling's forty-seven artillerymen, leaving the surviving men on the *Sachem* and the *Clifton* to become prisoners of war for the remainder of the conflict.

Old-time Christmas in Beaumont

Christmas in Beaumont a century ago wasn't the same as the holiday we know today, for then people observed customs that were similar yet different from the ones that we follow. Fortunately for us, Katie Lamb Moulton, a Beaumont native, left us her recollections of girlhood Christmases in the town.

"Christmas Gift!" was the greeting used universally in Beaumont the same way we today say "Merry Christmas!" According to Katie, everyone tried to greet each of their friends with this traditional Southern salutation before the other had a chance to shout out the words.

Katie recorded particular remembrances of the 1883 Christmas, for in that year one of her friends received as a present the most extraordinary doll she had ever seen. Indeed, the gift was one of the finest dolls Beaumont had ever known.

Named "Edie," the doll had a body made from kid leather and a bisque head with real hair. Katie greatly envied the recipient of the doll, one of her playmates named Louvie Burnham. Together Katie and Louvie dressed the doll in an elaborate bustled white wedding dress complete with three petticoats and lace trimmed drawers.

Katie so loved the doll that after her childhood playmate died many years later, her heirs gave the beloved doll to Katie. When interviewed in 1931, she declared, "I wouldn't part with dear old Edie for any consideration."

There were no Christmas trees in Beaumont in the early 1880s, according to Katie. The custom had not reached southeast Texas from centers of culture in the East. By the end of the decade, however, Katie remembered that a few trees had begun appearing in a handful of public places.

The Christmas trees provided a mechanism for gift exchanging among friends. Katie remembered that the gifts, unwrapped but labeled, were attached to the branches of the trees. On one instance, one of Katie's friends was given a pair of stockings with wide stripes running around them, and these were shown off to all the audience before being given to the embarrassed girl.

Caroling did not become a popular Christmastime activity in Beaumont until the turn of the century. Katie recalled that she was a member of the Beaumont Mandolin Club about 1901 or 1902 when it engaged in a novel experiment in caroling. The club consisted of about fifteen mostly young people who played mandolins, guitars, violins, or cellos. As the club members gathered to go out playing and singing Christmas songs, the leader arrived with a small Christmas tree decorated with candles and bearing small gifts for each member of the group. They took the miniature tree with them, sitting it on the porches of the houses where they played and sang, its candles providing the light.

With all the hustle and bustle of present-day Christmas parties, pell-mell gift shopping, sumptuous dinners, and constant bombardment by advertisements, one can only wonder whether we find any more pleasure from the holiday than did little Katie Lamb and Louvie Burnham with their wonderful doll in Beaumont of 1883.

The First Texas State Fair

For over a century and a quarter, Dallas has hosted the Texas State Fair, but it cannot claim the first such event. Much to the chagrin of the present-day Dallas promoters, the initial state fair of Texas took place almost four hundred miles away in Corpus Christi.

When the first Texas state fair was organized in Corpus in late 1851, the town was little more than a village fronting on the Gulf of Mexico. Its commercial district straggled along the beachfront, while the residential district overlooked it from the bluffs behind.

The town had come into being as a result of two factors: promotion by the townsite owner, Colonel Henry L. Kinney, and its fortunate location as a supply depot established by the U.S. Army in 1845 during the Mexican War. With the end of hostilities, most of the military activity declined, and the town almost withered away. The discovery of gold in California in 1848 brought an influx of transients headed for the Pacific, but they departed almost as soon as they had arrived on their way to the goldfields. With almost all his money invested in the Corpus area, Colonel Kinney decided that the best way to promote "his" town would be through a state fair.

As early as autumn 1851, Colonel Kinney began advertising for a special sale of livestock to take place at Corpus Christi on May 1, 1852. Soon the planned auction grew to become an exposition. Kinney sent twenty thousand printed handbills to all parts of the United States and abroad advertising what soon was dubbed the "Lone Star State Fair." These exaggerated brochures offered luxurious accommodations and lavish entertainments to any visitors who would come.

Among those who accepted the invitation was a correspondent from the New Orleans *Daily Delta*. One of the estimated two thousand guests who attended the May 1852 event, he sent reports back to the Crescent City about what he found.

"The lights are charming," the Louisianan wrote. "A fine sea breeze is always blowing, and the delightful band of music which plays every evening on the bluff at Col. Kinney's house adds to the enchantment of the moonlit scenery on the beautiful bay." Though Corpus Christi was still barely a village, scarcely able to accommodate its guests, the newspaperman predicted, "There is no doubt that Corpus must, in time, become a large town, and a place of great agricultural trade and commerce."

The principal exhibition area for the fair was in a large wareroom inside a brick store owned by Judge James Webb. The goods on display were mostly of Mexican manufacture, including saddles, blankets, bridles, spurs, and specimens of embroidery.

The most popular entertainment for most of the guests was beneath the big top at Maltby's Circus, which had traveled to Corpus Christi to be part of the fair. Each night the arena was crowded with visitors, who were awed by "Madame Ella Nunn . . . displaying her grace and skill in horsemanship."

Writing for his readers back home in New Orleans, the journalist penned that "I cannot do better than give you a description of the audience in order to give you an idea of the most singular combination of people here." The mixture of ethnic groups was representative of all of Texas at the time. "On the reserved seats are to be seen elegantly dressed American and Mexican ladies, flirting their fans with the same coquetry that they would at an opera." With them were U.S. Army officers, fashionable gentlemen in white kid gloves.

Adjacent to the genteel folk, the journalist observed the "frontiersmen of Texas," whom the reporter described as having "their fine-shooters in their belts, and the handle of a Bowie-knife peeping from their bosoms." Additionally the visitor saw Comanche and Lipan Apache Indians, Mexican rancheros, and a few Blacks.

The deportment of the fair goers greatly surprised the visitor. "What is remarkable here is that all the men from the frontier and interior of Texas go armed through the crowded streets, and yet, with the exception of a fisticuff row in a drinking shop, I have not yet heard of a single quarrel."

Thinking of Texans at fairs today, one would never expect the Louisianan to report, "they are the most quiet and orderly set of people I ever saw."

"Colorado" and the Corpus Christi Rodeo

Texans have always relished encounters between men and beasts, and such an event was staged at Corpus Christi in 1852.

In May 1852 Colonel Henry L. Kinney, the founder of Corpus Christi, organized the "Lone Star State Fair," the first state fair in Texas. Among the components of this fair were a Mexican bullfight and an equestrian event much akin to our modern rodeos. One particular animal took a prominent role in both competitions.

A correspondent from the New Orleans *Daily Delta* was among two thousand guests in Corpus Christi for the state fair, and on May 20 his newspaper published his report on the exposition. "This has been decidedly the most exciting week of the fair," the reporter began. "The sports of the week commenced with a bullfight, Camarena, the celebrated bullfighter of the City of Mexico taking the field."

A large crowd came to witness the encounter between man and animal. In the first two fights the bulls were badly wounded. Things then changed. "When they let in the little red bull, 'Colorado,'" the journalist reported, "Camarena found his match." Twice the bull nearly gored the well-known matador. "The little red bull was too much for him, and it was accordingly decided to make it a drawn fight."

"Colorado's" appearances were not yet over. He next came up in the rodeo. The Louisiana newspaperman described the proceeding as "a contest for superior horsemanship." The competition among riders began with an event similar to present-day bulldogging. "The first feat of agility," the correspondent wrote, "consisted of throwing a bull down while running at full speed." The bull was released from a pen and started down a road. The mounted competitor then would "dash after him, and coming up, catch him by the tail, and, by a sudden turn, as the animal would rise on his fore legs, would be thrown rolling on the ground." This was no small task.

For the audience, bull throwing was entertaining. "Sometimes the bull would make a sudden bolt from the road, just as the rider would be reaching for the bull's tail, and before he could recover himself, would measure his own length on the ground, to the great merriment of the crowd."

The next contest consisted of picking up a silver dollar from the ground at a full gallop on horseback. "This feat created great sport," the writer noted, "and loud cheers greeted the victor."

In the third and final rodeo event, "Colorado" the bull returned. "The next feat of dexterity was that of riding a wild bull," the correspondent reported, "and the little red bull, 'Colorado,' was turned loose for the occasion." Much more difficult than modern bull riding, "the feat is effected by a sudden spring from the ground, and many a hard fall did the competitors receive before any met with success." Eventually, one of the Mexican vaqueros somehow managed to clamber onto the back of "Colorado," and "such running, roaring and pitching as followed even made the mules laugh."

In this pioneer rodeo in Texas, "Colorado," the little red bull, was overwhelmingly the star.

Riding Out a Hurricane

Nowadays when tropical storms strike the Gulf Coast, residents have the choice of either fleeing inland or staying home to ride out the tempests. The option of escaping the storms is comparatively new. Only in recent years have weather forecasters been able to warn people that hurricanes were coming so that they could get out of harm's way.

Throughout the nineteenth century, hurricanes caught Gulf Coast residents without the warnings now taken for granted. This is precisely what happened to Aransas Pass harbor pilot John T. Mercer and his family in September 1875.

Fortunately Mercer kept a detailed daily journal, and five of its volumes, covering the years from 1866 to 1881, are preserved. They tell us much about life on the Texas Gulf Coast over a century ago, and they include a running narrative of events at Aransas Pass during one particular storm.

Mercer began his journal entry for Thursday, September 16, 1875, early in the morning. At one o'clock a.m., he wrote, "All hands got up. The wind blowing fearful from the north northwest." As the day progressed, the weather didn't improve.

In the darkness of the early morning hours, Mercer's sons went down to the bay and retrieved their rowboats. Later they tied them to a blacksmith shop building to keep them from being dashed to pieces by the wind. Already storm-buffeted vessels in the harbor were dragging anchor, some of them washing ashore. "The *Bessie* lays on her side," Mercer wrote, describing one of the wind-battered vessels he saw. "She appears to be fast to her anchor [and] she is catching fits. The *Farwell* is out of sight."

At home earnest preparations were under way for the worst case scenario. "Ned and Tom filled everything that would hold water, for fear the tide would get in the wells," Mercer penned.

Neither men nor animals could escape the fury of the winds. "Several chickens had the life blown out of them, roosting in the trees," Mercer wrote. It was hopeless for Mercer to try to cook the dead birds. He complained on the pages of his journal, "We tried to make a fire in the house, but the rain came down the chimney and put it out." Cooking was out of the question.

Despite the high winds and torrential rains, members of the harbor pilot's household continually attempted to secure their own and others' vessels in the harbor. One ship named the *Doaga* broke loose from its moorings, and several of the men went out in dingies to try to save it. "They taken the ballast out of her and moored her with part of it," Mercer scribbled, adding, "They had quite a job of it."

By six o'clock on the evening of the storm, Mercer was able to note in his journal that the wind was finally abating and the tide was falling. "I made out to make a fire in the house," he wrote. At least there would be a hot supper. After the meal, the diarist recorded, "All hands feel tired and wet," and everybody was headed for bed by 7 p.m.

Concluding his entry, Mercer observed, "This day beats anything for high water since the flood. All well, nobody hurt, thanks God."

One of La Salle's Murderers

Three centuries ago René-Robert Cavelier, Sieur de La Salle, the famous French explorer who first sailed the length of the Mississippi, was murdered in East Texas by his own men. One of the conspirators was sixteen-year-old Jean l'Archevêque, and it is his story that has intrigued me.

In July 1684 young l'Archevêque departed with La Salle's expedition, sailing from La Rochelle, France, with almost three hundred colonists bound for the mouth of the Mississippi to establish a French settlement. For reasons unknown, they overshot their destination and landed instead at Matagorda Bay on the Texas coast.

Moving inland to a site on Garcitas Creek northwest of present-day Point Comfort, the Frenchmen built Fort St. Louis for their protection. Their colonizing effort was a failure, however, and the settlement eventually deteriorated.

While in East Texas attempting to reach other French settlements on the Mississippi, La Salle fell victim to five of his own men on March 18, 1687. The conspirators first killed the explorer's nephew, servant, and a loyal Indian boy, bludgeoning them to death in their sleep with an axe. The next morning when La Salle came seeking his nephew, young l'Archevêque decoyed him into an ambush by telling him that his nephew was nearby on the river. Just after the leader passed the teenager, two assailants hidden in tall grass shot La Salle in the head. In mockery and insult, they stripped his body of its clothing and left it on the riverbank to be eaten by wild animals.

In time most of the colonists were either killed or taken captive by the Indians, but a handful successfully reached French Canada to tell the tale.

Jean l'Archevêque chose to live among the Indians, remaining there until Spanish explorer Alonso de León "rescued" him two years later in 1689. Spanish authorities took the young Frenchman, who was illegally in their domain, to Mexico and eventually to Spain for questioning, only to return him to Mexico in 1692. From there he joined a military expedition commanded by Don Diego de Vargas, which the next year recaptured New Mexico from rebellious Pueblo Indians.

A naturalized Spanish subject, l'Archevêque was now twenty-two years old, and he settled in Santa Fe. There he remained a soldier for a few years before becoming a trader. In 1697 he wedded Antonia Gutierrez, with her had a son and daughter, and additionally had another son with an Indian servant. The descendants still live in New

Mexico. After his first wife died, forty-eight-year-old Jean remarried on August 16, 1719.

L'Archevêque had hardly settled back into domestic life before he left on yet another expedition. This campaign, headed by Don Pedro de Villasur, departed Santa Fe on June 14, 1720. The forty Spaniards with Apache auxiliaries were destined for the plains hundreds of miles to the northeast, where French traders had become active and threatened Spanish sovereignty.

The expedition ended in disaster. Early on the morning of August 16, 1720, the first anniversary of l'Archevêque's remarriage, a large Pawnee Indian war party attacked and routed the encamped Spaniards thought to have been somewhere on the Platte River. Probably aided by French agents or traders, the Indians massacred all but about half a dozen escaping Spaniards.

Thirty-three years after the assassins left La Salle's corpse laying in the East Texas sun, l'Archevêque himself lay unburied on the prairie, killed by Frenchmen or their Indian allies. The score had been settled.

III.

HILL COUNTRY

FARMHOUSE NEAR ADAMSVILLE

Don Collins

A Lady's Life with Texas Bachelors

When newlywed Jane Lewis Maury came to Texas in the late 1870s, her first "real home" was on a ranch that her husband, Albert Maverick, had purchased on the Medina River northwest of San Antonio. There she found herself and her husband joining the company of Texas bachelors.

Albert had bought his Bandera County ranch from a Mr. Matt, who lived there with one John Gahagan, both of them Irishmen. The landscape there with post oaks and occasional large liveoaks, in Mrs. Maverick's words, "looked like a well kept park," but the home into which she moved did not necessarily look so inviting.

"The house was just what one might expect it to be—kept by two middle-aged bachelors," she noted. Mr. Matt, the former owner, she described as "a cranky Irishman." He was known to tie a red bandana around his head and run about the place with his quirt beating all the dogs whenever he came down with a headache.

Nervous and impatient with things beyond his control, Matt became irritated at even the sound of his own chickens. Mrs. Maverick noted that "when a hen would do her duty by laying an egg, her cackling would annoy him to such an extent he would rush out and throw stones until she quieted down." Every fall men had to go to the corn crib, where the hens roosted, and pick up a wagon load of stones that the irate Matt had thrown in order to make space for storing the new year's corn crop.

John Gahagan, the other bachelor, who remained at the ranch after Matt left for Galveston upon selling to the Mavericks, was a completely different sort of person. "He was a godsend to two greenhorns like we were," Mary Maverick wrote. A handsome man, he "rode a good horse and always wore a pistol and cartridge belt, high boots, high hat and a red handkerchief around his neck." Most importantly, he knew how to manage a ranch.

Mrs. Maverick's arrival created quite a stir not only among the bachelor residents but also among the animals, few of which had ever seen the profile of a woman in a dress. "I was the first woman to set foot on the Matt Ranch," she stated, "and when the chickens, dogs and stock of all kinds caught sight of me, the shock was too great and they took to the brush."

Being the lone female and feeling responsible for caring for her husband and the other men on the ranch, Mrs. Maverick found herself nearly helpless. She had grown up in Virginia and had always had black servants to do everything. "I did not know how to boil water," she declared.

Coming to her rescue was Mrs. Annie E. Brown, who lived in the vicinity and who became housekeeper at the ranch. As Mrs. Maverick recalled, "[she] came over and saved our lives." A genteel woman who had grown up in a banker uncle's New Orleans home, Annie Brown had become stranded in Texas almost twenty years before and had never left. As a remembrance of her happy girlhood, she always carried with her a special feather bed.

"I have had to work so many years," she explained to Mary Maverick, "I like to have some proof of better days." Alone on the Texas prairies, Annie Brown had the comfort of knowing "I carry my bed and sewed up on the inside are some little trophies of my youth." Even though she might be the housekeeper for rough bachelors on a Texas ranch, she always had part of home sewed up in her feathers and ticking.

Four Years in a Cave

Jap Brown, one of the best known bee hunters of Blanco County in the 1850s, spent four years hiding out in one of the many caves which abound in that area of the Texas Hill Country.

Brown and his family had moved to Blanco County and created a prosperous farm with a log home, outbuildings, cleared fields, and a variety of livestock. Living in the same area on the Blanco River were the Pierce, Hitchcock, and Star families, as well as several others. Many of the people made cash money by cutting cedar shingles and fence posts, which they sold easily in Austin.

When the Civil War began for Texans with secession in 1861, most of the members of the little Blanco County community stayed aloof from political agitation, only wanting to be left to themselves. The last thing that Jap Brown and his neighbors wanted was for any of the men to be drafted into anyone's army and be taken away from their families.

After the Confederate government instituted mandatory conscription into the army, draft agents began appearing in cities and rural communities across Texas to "recruit" men to serve in the military. Many Texans who opposed the war fled to Mexico, but some simply hid out, hoping to evade the conscription officers. Jap Brown decided to hide.

Being a bee hunter by vocation, Jap knew the limestone cliffs and caves of Blanco County probably better than any other man, and he picked out as a temporary home a big subterranean chamber that opened onto the cliffs of the Blanco River about a mile from his home. It was invisible from above its entrance, and it was barely perceptible from the bed of the river about fifty feet below.

Together with a neighbor, John C. Pierce, Brown created a comfortable retreat in which to wait out the war. For the two Texans, life in the cavernous depths was preferable to that of a conscript in the Confederate Army.

The local officials all knew that Brown and Pierce were hiding out, but they never could find them. For more than three years the conscription officers and home guard troops, known at the time as "Heel Flies," regularly circulated through the vicinity, exploring every canyon and mountaintop. They never could find a trace of Brown and Pierce, although they knew that the objects of their search were somewhere in nearby concealment.

Once the "Heel Flies" almost discovered the secluded retreat. Grandpa Pierce, a relative of Brown's companion, often carried food to the two draft evaders. On one occasion he started to the cave with a basket of food and a coffeepot, but his wife foresaw danger.

"I see death in that coffee pot and in that basket!" she declared. "Don't touch that coffee pot and don't take that basket; if you do, you will be betrayed!" Grandpa Pierce accordingly stuffed some corn pone and jerked beef into the front of his shirt and set off for the cave, his long walking stick in one hand.

As the old man ambled along, he sang out hog calls, a signal that Brown and Pierce understood. About halfway to his destination, the grandfather found himself surrounded by two dozen mounted home guards who demanded to know what he was doing.

"I am hunting my old bell sow," Grandpa Pierce replied. "Have you seen an old spotted sow with a bell on?" he asked. After a few more questions, the "Heel Flies" let Grandpa Pierce continue his quest for his "old belled sow," but he did not go any farther in the direction of the cave that day.

Mrs. Jap Brown was a thrifty woman who was well known for her household economy. Throughout the war, when many families were suffering material want, her family remained well clothed and fed.

After the war, when Brown and Pierce were able to return from hiding to their homes, it was learned that cotton and wool cards together with a spinning wheel had become part of their cavern furniture. The surprisingly large amounts of spun thread carried from their underground hiding place during the dark hours of the night contributed to the productivity that caused neighbors to marvel at how Mrs. Brown was able to make more cloth than any other two women in the country.

Beekeeping on the Texas Frontier

Noah Smithwick, one of the most reliable of the early Texans who recorded frontier experiences, left remembrances about many of his activities. Having not read through his book, *The Evolution of a State*, for quite a while, I picked it up to thumb through its pages the other day and came on his comments about Texas beekeeping 175 years ago. Judging from what he said, the old timer undoubtedly knew what he was talking about.

In the days of early settlement in the 1830s, frontiersmen discovered the locations of natural bee trees through using what they called "bee bait." They would take a container of honey from home and place it in a location likely to have bees, usually near where they could find water. Then they would wait, watching the bait for any bees it might attract.

When bees appeared at the vessel of honey, the frontiersmen waited until they "had filled their pouches and started for home." Then the settlers carefully noted the direction the bees took. "It being a well established fact that a laden bee flies in a 'bee line,' an expert had no difficulty in following them to their hive," which generally was in a hollow tree. This, Smithwick noted, was called "coursing" the bees.

After a hive of bees had been established at a farmstead, more hives could be established when in the spring the bee colonies divided. Smithwick described the phenomenon: "The young brood of bees, on arriving at maturity, are turned out by the heads of the hive to hustle for themselves." Creating quite a commotion, the bees ejected from the hive "buzz around at a great rate and finally settle down on some convenient limb to hold a council, perhaps to dispatch agents to look up new quarters."

At this point the alert beekeeper appeared to "hive" the swarm in a container that he provided in order to keep the colony on the property. "To prevent their escape we used to throw water on them to prevent their flying and beat on tin pans and raise a general hullabaloo." This noise drowned out the sound made by the queen bee, so her minions went inside the keeper's container, leaving her to follow them inside.

The hives that the settlers most often used for their bees were sections of hollow tree trunks with planks nailed across the top. To rob such a hive of its honey, "we pried off the board and smoked the bees out with burning rags."

Smithwick noted that the methods used were primitive but effective. The smoke from the burning rags "did not tend to improve the flavor of the honey," he said, "but we were not fastidious in small matters, and fortunate indeed was the robber who escaped without stings."

German Captive of the Indians

In the little cemetery just outside Loyal Valley in Mason County, Texas, stands a low granite marker inscribed with the name, Herman Lehmann, and the dates, 1859–1932. There's nothing unusual about the tombstone, but the man whose remains lie beneath it was indeed unusual.

Herman Lehmann was the most famous of all the nineteenth-century Texas German captives of the Plains Indians. Herman was captured northwest of Fredericksburg by a party of raiding Apache Indians on May 16, 1870. In his autobiography, published in 1927, Herman recalled that on the eventful day he, his two sisters, and a brother had been sent into a wheat field near the family's cabin "to scare the birds away." They sat down in the field to play, "and the first thing we knew we were surrounded by Indians," he said.

One of the warriors grabbed Herman and carried him away, but not without a fight. Herman later recalled, "I locked my fingers in his long black hair and pulled as hard as I could; I kicked him in the stomach; I bit him with my teeth."

It was all to no avail, for the warrior succeeded in forcing Herman to accompany him. For the next nine years Lehmann lived first as a captive of the Apaches and then with the Comanches, growing up as a Plains Indian. He became a warrior in both tribes, participating as a warrior on numerous Indian raids into Texas and Mexico with war parties from both Apache and Comanche tribes.

Concerning one such incident, Herman recalled, "Springtime came on apace, and when the weather got warm we made a raid down into the settlements for horses." Going into Mason County, "we came upon a herd of horses." There they found also "a man . . . pretending to guard them, but he was fast asleep." He continued, "We drove an arrow through him, and this aroused him for a few minutes; then he turned over into a sleep from which no man can awaken. We scalped him and drove off the horses."

On at least one occasion Herman returned on a raid to his immediate home country. "The band to which I belonged went down into the settlements around Fredericksburg," he remembered. Once they looked through the windows of a building "and there we saw some men in a saloon drinking beer." Lehmann continued, "We let them drink in peace, but we took charge of all the horses we could find."

In 1879 U.S. military authorities returned Herman Lehmann from the Indians to his family, which by then was living at Loyal Valley. There Lehmann remained for the remainder of his life.

The former captive relearned German speech, married, and had a family, but to the end of his days he kept close ties with his friends among the Plains Indians on the reservations. There he officially was enrolled by the U.S. government "with full rights as a member of the Comanche tribe."

War Parties and Locomotives

Herman Lehmann, who spent most of his later life living in Mason and Gillespie counties, was probably the best known of all the Texas captives of the Indians. He spent almost all his adolescence, nine years from 1870 to 1879, living with the Apache and Comanche Indians.

As an eleven year old, Herman was captured by a war party outside his family's cabin about twenty-five miles northwest of Fredericksburg, Texas. He subsequently became acculturated to the lifestyle of the nomadic Plains Indians.

As a warrior and war party member, Herman even raided his own childhood neighborhood. On one occasion he and other warriors went into the very town of Fredericksburg. They went up on the hill north of town and then, as Herman reminisced, "I went into a man's lot and got two good horses, and my companions captured a nice herd nearby." Next they proceeded northward, some of them taking the main road and others exploring the country on either side for livestock they might steal. "We got several good mules from one of my old neighbors, Fritz Ellenbracht," he later recalled.

While on one of his raids into the Texas settlements, Herman saw his first steam railway locomotive. Herman's war party had come to the Hill Country; Herman later believed that the location was somewhere near Austin. On that occasion while they were waiting in a ravine for the moon to come up and give them light for raiding, "a train came suddenly around a curve from behind a mountain and was right on us before we had time to mount our horses."

The locomotive terrified the unsuspecting warriors. "That hideous monster, belching smoke and hissing steam, and with glaring lights, bore down upon us at a terrific speed." Completely routed, "we ran, scrambling over rocks and through the brush to get away." The train seemed to the Indians to be following them. They decided that it must have lost their trail, though, because "it went rushing on away from us."

Herman remembered, "I was uneasy for fear the awful thing had caught three of our comrades." When one of the warriors gave the assembly signal, however, the missing men appeared from hiding.

The members of the war party held a consultation about what they had seen and what they should do in response. "We decided to leave that region at once and not to attempt to steal any horses there," Herman related, "for that monster might return and catch us."

Rebels versus Kickapoos on Dove Creek

It sounds a little unlikely to consider a major fight between Confederate forces and the Kickapoo Indians in West Texas during the Civil War, but that's just what happened in early 1865. The story of what became a notable rebel defeat in Texas began just a few days before.

On December 9, 1864, a group of Confederate frontier defense forces from Erath County, Texas, discovered the abandoned camp from several hundred Indians on the Clear Fork of the Brazos about thirty miles above Fort Phantom Hill. Militia commander N. M. Gillintine reported, "I found a camp of a large party of Indians, 92 wigwams & the poles of ten tents."

If Gillintine had been worth his salt as a frontiersman, he would have realized that the camp consisting of wood and brush wigwams did not belong to the warlike Comanche, Kiowa, or Apache Indians, but rather to the generally peaceable woodland Indians from the East. The distinction seemingly was lost on Gillintine. That day he wrote a dispatch back to his superiors asking, "I wish you to come, and fetch a sufficient number of men with you." Gillintine was out to fight Indians—any Indians.

In response to the request, both regular Confederate Army troops and state frontier militia forces headed westward about Christmastime

1864, making a rendezvous with Gillintine and his two dozen men. Altogether they had over 450 men.

Finding the Indians camped southeast of present-day San Angelo on Dove Creek, an intermittent tributary of Spring Creek, the Southerners divided their forces between regulars and the militia, each group attacking the Indians from an opposite direction. The results of the fight on January 8, 1865, were disastrous to the Texans.

Having left the Mississippi Valley on a trek to Mexico, the contingent of woodland Indians had camped on Dove Creek in an easily defendable position. One of the militia commanders, S. S. Totton, reported, "The Indians were . . . in a dense thicket of green briars and live oak, containing about 100 acres."

After repulsing attacks by the regulars on one side and the militia on the other, the Kickapoos counterattacked. They fought the better part of the day against the regular troops, recovering their horse herd which the soldiers had taken early in the encounter.

The frontier militia troops, on the other hand, stood up to the Kickapoos for only a few minutes. After they had dismounted from their horses, waded knee-deep into Dove Creek, and attacked the camp, its defenders routed the Texan Indian fighters. One of the rebels later reported, "The militia was thrown into panic and fled like stampeded cattle."

By the end of the day, the Kickapoo camp was again quiet, the Confederate troops and Texas militia having been driven from the field of battle. After the casualties were counted, the Indians had lost about a dozen killed while the rebels had lost twenty-two killed and nineteen wounded.

Having attacked a completely peaceable party of eastern, woodland Indians, which they never even attempted to identify, the Confederates found themselves soundly whipped. This time they probably deserved it.

"Remarkably Good Marksmanship" on the Nueces

There are not too many stories about groups of Texans killing other groups of Texans, but one such incident took place on the Nueces

River on August 10, 1862. One party attacked and killed as many as nineteen of its fellow Texans, losing at least two of its own number in the process.

The secession of Texas from the Union and the start of the Civil War prompted the so-called "Battle of the Nueces." Many Texans opposed secession and war, Texas being the only state in the Confederacy in which citizens actually voted on whether or not to leave the Union. The majority of the electorate chose to support the South, but many disagreed. A considerable number of these opponents were German immigrants living in the Hill Country.

After Texas had joined the Southern Confederacy and the war had begun, a party of sixty-five young men from the Fredericksburg area decided that they would be wise to leave the state. Comprised mostly of Germans, they headed southwestward toward Mexico, where some of them planned to wait out the war and where others proposed joining the U.S. Army if they could. One of the latter was Henry Schwelthelm, a twenty-one-year-old immigrant from Düsseldorf, Germany.

The pro-Union Texans departed their Hill Country homes about August 1, 1862, meeting at a pre-determined location on Turtle Creek west of Kerrville. They elected Fritz Tegener as their leader, and then they proceeded in a leisurely manner toward the Mexican border, shooting abundant wild game along the way. Making only five to ten miles daily, the party reached the vicinity of the Nueces by August 9. There they pitched camp in a beautiful setting that Schwelthelm remembered as having plenty of grass and water but no real protection.

Unknown to the young German Texans, a detachment of about 125 Texas Confederates under the command of Lieutenant C. D. McRae had been on their trail, catching up on the evening of the August 9. The next morning the unsuspecting Germans awakened to the sound of gunfire and the cry remembered by Schwelthelm: "Charge them, boys, charge them! Give them H--l!"

The rebel troops attacked from the shelter of thick cedar clumps, while the Unionist civilians defended themselves mostly in the open. The result of the hour-long fight was a slaughter in which nineteen Unionists were killed but only two rebels lost their lives. The remainder of the young German Texans scattered, some returning home and other continuing on to Mexico.

Henry Schwelthelm was one who did indeed continue on into Mexico, on the way there accidentally stumbling into some of McRae's men under the command of an officer named Duff. They were escorting Dr. Downs, the post surgeon from Fort Clark, back from caring for the Confederate wounded on the Nueces.

In the conversation with the Southerners, Schwelthelm learned that when the surgeon asked about dressing the wounds of some of the pro-Union civilians, the rebels told him, "Never mind, we will attend to them." Schwelthelm reported that he later learned that the Confederates had gone onto the battleground and shot every wounded man in the head, giving rise to later reports of "remarkably good marksmanship" by the rebel troops.

Courageous Action on the Pecos

On the west bank of Las Moras Creek a couple of miles south of Brackettville at the side of Farm to Market Road 3348 stands an unpretentious little country cemetery. The entry is marked by a metal gate, and you can see a flag pole. In many ways, it is like hundreds of other rural graveyards, but in one way it differs.

Everywhere you look in the graveyard stand white marble slabs denoting the graves of veterans. When you read them you find tombstone after tombstone marked, "Congressional Medal of Honor." This is no everyday cemetery.

The veterans buried here were all members of a military unit known as the Seminole Negro scouts of the U.S. Army, their family members, or their descendants. The mixed Black and Native American scouts initially were recruited from both Texas and Mexico in the summer of 1870, but their actual origin was in Florida, Alabama, or the Indian Territory. The Seminole Indians and escaped Black slaves had lived in the southeastern United States many years until they were expelled to Oklahoma and the West by President Andrew Jackson in the early nineteenth century.

The mixed Black and Seminole warriors were widely known for their exceptional abilities in trailing either people or animals. Consequently they were selected to form the special unit of scouts in 1870 to aid regular troops defending the frontier against Apache and Comanche raiders. The War Department furnished the Seminole Negro scouts with arms, ammunition, and rations, while the men provided their own horses. Rarely wanting to wear strict military uniforms, the scouts added their own civilian and Native American elements to their dress.

Noted during the nineteenth century as "excellent hunters and trailers, and brave scouts . . . splendid fighters," the Seminole Negro scouts participated in dozens of engagements against hostile Indians in the Rio Grande country for the next decade and a half, although the unit survived until 1914. One of the many such encounters took place at the Eagle's Nest Crossing of the Pecos River on April 25, 1875.

Lieutenant John L. Bullis, commander of the scouts, with a sergeant, a bugler, and a trooper had trailed about seventy-five stolen horses to the crossing, where they came upon the twenty-five to thirty Comanche warriors who had taken them in Texas. The four men secured their horses and crept around to a hidden position about seventy-five yards from the thieves who were attempting to cross the stock to the other side of the river. Bullis and the scouts opened fire on the miscreants, maintaining the fight for about forty-five minutes, and in the process they killed three Comanches, wounded a fourth, and drove them away from the stolen herd twice.

Eventually the warriors realized that their attackers were so few in number. They worked their way around behind the scouts' position and opened up with Winchester repeating rifles. Greatly outgunned, Bullis and his men had to retreat, hoping to escape with their lives.

The three scouts reached their mounts and began galloping away when Sergeant John Ward looked back to see Bullis still afoot. His partially trained young horse had broken away in the excitement, leaving the Comanches to close in on the commander. "We can't leave the lieutenant, boys," Ward cried out as he wheeled his mount around and charged back, the others following on his heels.

The warriors opened furious fire on the three rescuers, especially on Sergeant Ward. One of their bullets cut Ward's carbine sling, and as he reached down to help Bullis onto his horse behind him, another shot shattered the stock of the gun. In the meantime, the bugler and the trooper began firing as rapidly as they could with their single-shot Sharps carbines, keeping the warriors back from Ward and Bullis. Shooting to sides and rear, they managed to provide a successful rear guard action as all four men retreated from the field of battle.

Bullis summarized the action with the acknowledgment that the three Seminole Negro scouts "saved my hair," but the U.S. government recognized the heroism in a more tangible way. It gave all three scouts Congressional Medals of Honor that to this day are recognized on the grave markers that still stand at the little cemetery south of Brackettville.

On a Horse Thief's Trail

Known to his friends as "Old Sleuth," P. C. Baird of Mason County was one of the best known lawmen in late-nineteenth-century Texas. He was especially noted for his uncanny ability to trail and then capture bad men.

In a typical incident, not long after Baird had moved to Mason in the 1880s, Mr. William Schuessler about nine o'clock one August evening found his horse and saddle missing from outside the local Methodist church. The next morning he reported the loss to the local authorities, noting that he had just had the animal shod and describing the specific pattern of its new shoes. The distinctive tracks from the new shoes would make the mount comparatively easy to trail.

Sheriff John C. Butler assigned Deputy Baird to try to find the horse, and Baird immediately started looking for the specific tracks in the dirt of the roads leading out of Mason. He found the tracks leaving town on the road to Brady, but in about twelve miles the trail headed overland to the town of Eden.

About one and a quarter centuries ago Eden consisted of little more than a store, a post office, and a few scattered houses, but there the thief stopped to eat and to feed his horse. Baird discovered that "the postmistress, a small, slender, blackeyed woman, with an eye of an eagle, had scrutinized this 'gentleman horse thief' closely, and was able to give me a very accurate description of him, being the first person in my chase that had seen, or could give me any information concerning the rider of the horse." The postmistress hadn't seen the horse, but for Baird this made no difference "as I had the trail and track."

From Eden the thief continued out the San Angelo-Paint Rock road, but at the forks leading to the two different towns, Baird had trouble following his quarry because of a multitude of horse and cattle tracks. Finally he found a clear track leading down the Paint Rock branch. Following the road on beyond Paint Rock into Runnels City (the predecessor of present-day Ballinger), Baird rode into a livery stable to leave his wearied mount and to rent another to continue his search.

"It was about one o'clock in the afternoon," Baird remembered, and "to my surprise I found Mr. Schuessler's saddle hanging on a rack." The thief had traded it to the proprietor the day before for fifteen dollars and a cheaper saddle. Obviously he was in need of funds.

After a hasty lunch and a cup of coffee, Baird continued his pursuit, following the tracks northward over the trail about forty miles toward Abilene, Texas. Arriving on the outskirts that evening, the lawman unsaddled his horse, tied it to a mesquite tree, and lay down with his head on his saddle for a night's repose.

Just at first light the next morning, Baird rode on into Abilene, leaving his horse at the first livery stable he came to. He walked along the ends of the stalls but failed to find the stolen mount. The owner then told him that there were two more liveries in the town, so the deputy headed on. "I proceeded to the next barn just north of the railroad," Baird said. There, in an establishment owned by John B. Bell, he cast his eyes down the aisle into the stalls and found the horse that he had been trailing.

"I asked what such a horse was worth," Baird stated. The livery owner replied that the animal was not for sale, that he had just bought the horse and saddle for twenty-five dollars. "I said it was cheap, provided it was good property, . . . and . . . I then informed him that the horse was a stolen horse, and that I was an officer," Baird reported.

The lawman then learned that the man who had sold the horse was still in town but that he might be leaving on any of the several Texas & Pacific Railway trains that would pass through Abilene that day.

"About this time the breakfast bells began ringing," Baird said, so with his stomach growling he walked across the street to a restaurant "with my eyes open for my man." Just as he entered the eating place, Baird spotted his "much trailed and coveted prize" as he sat in front of a sumptuous breakfast. Baird remembered, "He appeared to recognize me and began rising from the table as if to make his way to an exit" when the lawman advised him not to be in any haste but to finish his meal. "You have not only got me—but my appetite also," the gentleman horse thief declared.

After he had eaten what he could, Baird led the thief to the local jail to allow the lawman to process his paperwork on the arrest. After a day, Baird escorted the man on horseback back to Mason. "Here I made another deposit for Sheriff Butler," Deputy Baird concluded. Another lawbreaker had been brought to justice.

A Freedman's Memories

For decades Tom Sullivan of Pearsall, Texas, kept listeners spellbound with his stories of life on the fringe of the South Texas brush country, once one of the roughest parts of Texas.

Born in servitude in Virginia about 1825, his entire family was stolen by slave kidnappers when he was five and a half years old. "They drove around in two or three states and finally went to Mississippi and hid us out for two years." The hiding place was on Tubby Creek in Monroe County.

"Finally, all of us but my father was sold to a man named Aaron Redus and my father was sold to Mr. Redus's son-in-law," Sullivan stated. "When Mr. Redus died we became property of his son, Bill, and I belonged to him until I was set free by emancipation."

Redus moved from Mississippi to Texas in 1848 or 1849, bringing with him his slave property, including Tom Sullivan. They all settled at Redus's new property on Hondo Creek in Medina County. There the slave had several encounters with members of raiding Indian war parties.

The end of slavery in Texas following the Confederate surrender at Appomattox brought dramatic changes for Tom Sullivan. For the first time he could make decisions about his own life. He soon became caught up in events greater than he might have imagined only a few months before.

Under the Reconstruction government after the Civil War, the former slave to his own great surprise was appointed deputy sheriff of Medina County. As part of a state effort to replace county officials who had been elected under the initial Reconstruction government, Sullivan was appointed by a district judge and a district attorney who had both been officers in the Union Army. The ex-slave remembered that the two government functionaries "stayed around a long time trying to find someone they could put in office. Finally they . . . elected me as deputy." Sullivan reluctantly accepted when the two unionists explained: "They said I had to serve whether I wanted to or not, as one of the deputies had to be a Colored man."

In the years that followed the war, Sullivan entered the lucrative freight business between shallow-water ports on the Gulf of Mexico and San Antonio. On the cart road, the hazards included cow skinners and robbers.

"Cow skinners was sure bad in those days," Sullivan remembered. These thugs would kill anyone's cattle just for their hides. "I've seen thousands of carcasses on the prairie north of Yorktown, where the skinners had killed them," the freedman said. Not all the skinners escaped with their raw hides, Sullivan related. "I once saw the bodies of three men hanging from an oak tree down there who had been hanged by the vigilantes."

In an especially vivid memory, Sullivan stated that once the vigilantes caught a cow skinner red-handed at his thievery. As the freedman remembered, "They killed him, cut the cow's paunch open and stuck the man's head in and then put up a sign warning other skinners that they would be done the same way."

Madman on the Medina

Today it is not uncommon for women to fear being caught at home with a mentally deranged intruder, but one rarely thinks about this occurring in the past. This is, however, precisely what happened to Annie E. Brown about 150 years ago, and she never forgot.

Born in Louisiana in 1838, Annie Brown had come to Texas with her husband about 1859. During the Civil War years from 1861 to 1865, Mr. Brown hauled cotton between San Antonio and the Mexican border as one of the ways that the Confederate authorities could avoid the Union naval blockade of the coasts and still export their cotton for foreign exchange. During much of this time Mrs. Brown lived with her baby daughter while working as a maid in the home of Christian Santelben of Castroville, Texas, on the Medina River just west of San Antonio.

One day, while her baby was on the bed, Mrs. Brown looked up to see a strange man without announcement enter the house and address her in German. "I replied that I could not speak that language, but would call the lady of the house, who would talk to him." The odd-acting man, who she had never seen before, "uttered an oath" and declared: "I can talk as good English as you." Mrs. Brown assumed that he was merely drunk.

In the meantime Mrs. Santelben, who had been sick in the bed, entered the room and asked what the man wanted. He replied, "My mission in life is to make angels for God." He thereupon drew a long knife and held it above the baby. Both women came to the realization that the intruder was not drunk at all—he was a lunatic . . . and they were at his mercy.

With remarkable presence of mind, Mrs. Santelben told the stranger: "You cannot make angels unless you first take the sacrament. Come, and I will give you bread and wine." He followed her into the kitchen, where she prepared something for him to eat.

In this interval Annie Brown took her little daughter and Mrs. Santelben's daughter, Mary, through an open window in the back of the house, and they hid for a time in an adjacent cornfield. "I could not bear to leave the old lady alone with that crazy man," Annie reported, "so giving the baby to Mary, I told her to go to the nearest neighbor for help." She then returned to the house.

There the intruder, still eating his food, seemed to have forgotten about the infant. Leaving him with the food, Mrs. Santelben and Annie Brown quietly exited the house together, going out onto a slightly wooded prairie from which point they could view what next took place. "We were afraid he would set fire to the house," she remembered.

Finally the man came out, spotted the two women in the pasture, drew his knife again and headed for them. The weak Mrs. Santelben stumbled several times as the women fled, but Annie Brown managed to help her across the field to a safe hiding place in an arroyo. "Not finding us, he went on down the road toward San Antonio," she related.

The help sent for never came, because during the war most of the adult men were off fighting Yankees, leaving only children, old men, and women at home. There was no one available to come to the women's aid.

A few days later Annie Brown learned that the crazy man had indeed gone on to San Antonio. There he entered a home, turned a table upside down and declared his mission "to make angels for God." It took eight officers of the law to subdue him, so the two ladies from Castroville felt good about their escape due to their fast thinking.

Keeping Quiet at Williams Ranch

At a bend in the county road about halfway between Goldthwaite and Mullin in Mills County stands the Williams Ranch Cemetery. Other than the ruins of former homes, this is about all that remains from a town that just over a century ago boasted 250 residents.

Why did the town die? It suffered from the self-inflicted wounds of a long and bloody feud among its inhabitants. It killed itself.

The Williams Ranch community came into existence in 1855 when a rancher named John Williams, on his way westward, camped at large springs that once flowed on Herd Pen Branch of Mullin Creek. He decided that the place would make a good home and he decided to stay.

One of the Williams sons established a grist mill on the creek, and this business formed the nucleus for the town. By 1880 it had grown to have several saloons, a drug store, a general mercantile, a blacksmith shop, a livery stable, a school, and two church congregations.

After the Civil War, the quarrels which led to the demise of Williams Ranch began with the mysterious killing of a man who had aided a teenaged girl to elope with an older suitor. While riding a five hundred dollar racehorse, the man and then his mount were killed by unknown assailants. Recriminations followed accusations, the residents of the community taking sides and forming two groups, the Honest Man's Club and the Trigger Mountain Mob.

Both good and bad men comprised the two parties, but a violent hatred soon sprang up among the former friends composing the secret groups. No one in Williams Ranch or its surrounding area could feel safe.

R. D. Forsythe, who survived the violence, later asserted to writer Tevis Clyde Smith that as many as a hundred men lost their lives in the subsequent strife. "Most of them were victims of ambuscades," he said, adding that "neither side gave the men they were after a chance to defend themselves."

In a representative incident, a man named Ace Brown organized a posse to try to find a friend of his named Smith who had disappeared. After spending several days looking for the missing man, the posse turned on Brown, who they decided had killed Smith and then assembled the search party to divert suspicions. A few days later people from Williams Ranch found Brown hanging from a tree in a thicket, but no one ever learned whether he had been involved in the disappearance of Smith.

The only way for a private citizen to survive at Williams Ranch was to see nothing, hear nothing, and say nothing. Henry Williams, grandson of town founder John Williams, reported, "The smart thing to do was to . . . tend your own business, and keep your mouth shut."

Another local resident told the following story to illustrate the point. "I was stopped one night as I was crossing a creek," he related.

As he started up the bank, a party of masked men in the darkness rode up to him, two holding his horse and the others surrounding his buggy. “One of them struck a match and held it close to my face,” he said, “asking me what I was doing there.” He answered their questions, knowing that he was in the hands of one or the other of the two factions. “One of them told me to go on into town, and keep my mouth shut,” and that he did.

For a long time thereafter, people would approach the man and attempt to draw out details about the incident, but he steadfastly refused to say anything. “I always played dumb,” he said.

Then twenty years later, in the course of a conversation with a friend on a totally different subject, the associate stopped, turned squarely toward him and said, “You sure know how to keep your mouth shut.” The friend placed his hand on the man’s shoulder, looked into his eye, and heard the response, “Yes, I do.”

The Pig War in Austin

Tempers were hot in Austin during the early spring of 1841, for the “Pig War” had reached its height. The affray was more than a dispute among neighbors, for it grew to become a major diplomatic incident between the Republic of Texas and the Kingdom of France.

On March 25, 1841, the French consular representative to Texas, Dubois de Saligny, wrote from Austin back to Paris that “France has just been insulted afresh in this city in the most outrageous manner.” In these words he began describing one of several encounters that he had had with his former landlord, Richard Bullock.

On this particular occasion in the front yard of George H. Flood, the charge d’affaires of the United States to Texas, Bullock accosted and threatened de Saligny with bodily harm if he would not settle up an unpaid hotel bill and compensate him for the loss of several of his hogs that de Saligny’s servant had killed. The innkeeper grabbed the Frenchman by his collar, shook him, and declared, “The next time that you come here, I will beat you to death.”

The difficulties between Bullock and de Saligny had begun months earlier in July 1840, when the diplomat first arrived in Austin. The Frenchman sought lodging in Bullock's hotel, where he and his servants spent a few nights before moving into a nearby private residence. De Saligny unfortunately failed to notify Bullock of his plans to move, and the hotel keeper proceeded to bill him for a month of lodging and food expenses for the diplomat, two of his servants, and "the negress (Rosanna)," Although the total bill later was reduced through arbitration to $323.75, the Frenchman never paid it, instead calling innkeeper Bullock "a cheat and a bully."

The default on payment of the hotel bill set the stage for the next phase in the hostilities.

Innkeeper Bullock kept his own herd of domestic swine, a ready source of fresh pork for his hotel. Many other Austin residents did the same, and herds of hogs roamed the city streets seeking whatever forage they might find.

Bullock's hogs began frequenting the stable adjoining the house leased by Dubois de Saligny, and the swine became an increasing nuisance. On March 21, 1841, the French diplomat complained to Jeames S. Mayfield, the Texas Secretary of State, saying:

> For a long time I have been annoyed, and I am still annoyed, by the numerous pigs with which the city is infested. Every morning one of my servants has to spend two hours repairing and nailing up the rails of the fence that these animals trample down to get at the corn for my horses.

Things grew worse. The diplomat protested further: "One day three pigs even penetrated to my bedroom and ate my linen and destroyed my papers."

So, what did the Frenchman do?

"I ordered one of the people in my household to kill any pig that came in my courtyard. . . . As a result of my orders, five or six pigs, apparently, were killed in my courtyard."

Richard Bullock, viewing the incident from his side of the fence, almented to the authorities that "between fifteen and twenty" of his hogs had been "maliciously and wantonly killed with pitchforks and pistols."

The Frenchman asserted to Secretary of State Mayfield that the laws of nations affording protection to diplomats and their households had been violated, and he refused to pay his accumulated hotel bill or to compensate Bullock for the loss of his swine.

Texan authorities balked at de Saligny's demand that they take summary action against Bullock. Instead they followed due process of law and tried him in court. De Saligny took offense at what he considered to be slow response to his difficulties and rashly broke off diplomatic relations between France and Texas.

The Pig War had effects far broader than might be expected, for de Saligny's brother-in-law was no less than Jean-Georges Humann, the minister of finances for France. For months Texan representatives in Paris had been attempting to negotiate a five million dollar loan from France, but their efforts were sabotaged by negative recommendations from de Saligny—all over an overdue hotel bill and the rooting of hogs.

Bread Loaves for a Bandana

An unlikely crew headed northwest from Brushy Creek near Austin in June 1841. It consisted of Republic of Texas soldiers, a contingent of merchants with wagons loaded with goods, and an assortment of hangers on. The 320-odd men called themselves the Texan Santa Fe Pioneers.

Participants in a project promoted by Texas president Mirabeau B. Lamar, the expedition members had inconsistent goals of opening overland trade between Santa Fe and Texas while at the same time extending Texas political authority to the lands of present-day eastern New Mexico east of the Rio Grande.

By the time that the "pioneers" had reached the plains east of Santa Fe, they were a threadbare, hungry, and motley band. Mexican military forces from the provincial capital in Santa Fe had no difficulty intimidating the Texans into surrender, whereupon the captives were marched down the Rio Grande and into the interior of Mexico for imprisonment that lasted well over a year.

One of the Texan Santa Fe pioneers was Cayton Erhard, a German immigrant who had grown up in Bastrop. When he returned to Texas from Mexican prisons in March 1843, he settled in San Marcos, where he became the first postmaster. Four decades later Erhard began writing a series of weekly articles about his early experiences for the *San Marcos Free Press*, and in the paper for March 8, 1883, I found the story of Erhard's trade of a bandana for five loaves of bread.

One night shortly after the Texans were captured in New Mexico, Erhard wandered away from his comrades. "Partly from loneliness," he wrote, "[I] strayed out of our prescribed limits, and it being pretty dark, I accidentally came up to one of our [Mexican] guard." Both Erhard and the sentry must have been pretty inoffensive, for in the dark of the night they struck up a "conversation" in sign language since neither could understand the others speech.

"He discovered that I had my head covered with a large gingham handkerchief and he took a fancy to it." Through gestures the Mexican guard communicated to the German immigrant teenager that he would trade him five loaves of bread for the bandana. Erhard jumped at the idea of getting something more to eat, for rations had been scanty at best.

"Here arose another quandry in my mind," Erhard reported. "I did not know the sentry, nor did he me, for dark it was." The Mexican resolved the problem of how to undertake the trade: "He motioned me to stand where he was, and he gave me his musket to stand guard in his place, signing that he would go to his camp and bring the bread." Thus, unknown to anyone else, Erhard became a guard for his own fellow Texans.

No sooner did one problem resolve itself than another arose. It was the custom for the Mexican sentries in a slow sequence to call out loud the words in Spanish, *sentinela alerta*, or "sentinel alert." "This dismal sentence would start perhaps a mile off, the next sentinel would repeat it in a few minutes afterwards, till it went all the round," Erhard remembered.

As he stood guard in place of the Mexican who was going for the bread, Erhard heard the *sentinela alerta* coming his direction. "I heard that doleful watchword coming near me; it soon would have been time for me to repeat it." Knowing that his Texas German brogue would be an absolute giveaway if he tried to repeat the two Spanish words, Erhard stood in complete fear. "But," as he later related, "my man came in time, he gave me five large hard loaves of bread [and] I snatched my handkerchief off my head and gave it to him."

"I made my way to camp," Erhard reported, "and after eating part of the bread, and saving the balance for next day, I went soundly and happily to sleep."

A Trail Driver's Remembrances

From his "'teenth year," the age thirteen, Ben Drake helped drive Texas cattle northward to markets in Kansas and beyond. Fortunately for us, Cora Melton Cross interviewed him as an older man and published her notes in the Dallas *Semi-Weekly Farm News* in 1927.

Drake's first drive was in 1871 from his home area south of Austin to Abilene, Kansas. The herd consisted of 2,800 longhorns belonging to Tid and Kinney Murchison. On the way the cowboys encountered a thunderstorm which broke all local records for the size of hailstones. "The storm impressed me so . . . that I determined, if I ever got home again, I would stay," Drake said. Then, however, he changed his mind. "When we got to Abilene and I had seen the sights and started on the trip back, I lined up for the next drive Murchison was to make." The puncher over the next nine years made a total of seven trips northward with Texan cattle.

Ben Drake's final experience on the trail came in 1879. This trip was the wettest that he had undergone, "We ran into heavy rains . . . in the Indian Territory. Couldn't keep a fire burning to cook a meal of victuals for two days," he remembered. "No grub ever will taste as good as that breakfast the morning of the third day when we broke our fast."

It was on this last drive that Drake suffered gunshots in his stomach and leg. "The boss took me to an Indian camp," he related. There the cowboy found himself placed in the hands of a small band of Indians for care.

"There were nine Indians . . . all living in two tents," the Texan later reported. All of them moved into one teepee, while they fitted up the other for their unexpected injured guest. The leader then doctored Drake according to Native American procedures, for there was no other medical care available. "I fared like they did," he said. "When they ate so did I, if they starved I did likewise."

Finally after Drake had begun hobbling around on crutches, the leader of the band notified U.S. government authorities and a federal marshal accompanied him back to Texas.

"I started in all over again helping with the stock and the farm, for I knew my trailing days were over," he stated. The cowman realized that "with a lame leg" he would never again ride bucking horses.

Looking back over his career first as a trail driving cowboy and then later as a farmer, Ben Drake reflected: "It has been pretty tough for me to just potter around instead of running my pony lickety-split like I used to do. But I will never forget the old trail driving days when, boy as I was, I rode and drove, drank black coffee, ate camp chuck and slept on a slicker in the rain as sound as if I had been lyin' on a feather bed."

Ben Thompson's Tombstone

Just over a century ago, Luke Watts was a moderately successful traveling salesman in the Austin/San Antonio area, but he didn't sell typical merchandise. He took orders for tombstones.

Watts forwarded his orders to a stonecutting firm that prepared the sepulchral monuments and then shipped them back to the customers. From town to town in his wagon he carried a few samples, on occasion selling them and chiseling the inscriptions himself.

On one evening Watts drove in to Austin from San Marcos and New Braunfels, where he had collected on several sales and received a number of new orders. He left his horse and wagon at Beat's Wagon Yard and headed for one of his favorite capital city haunts—the Iron Front Saloon.

At the Iron Front, the salesman bought a round of drinks for all in the house and then went upstairs to join in the gaming that took place there. No sooner had Watts begun some serious gambling than was he joined at the table by Ben Thompson. A gunman of considerable repute, Thompson had served as the city marshal of Austin, but by this time was making his living as a fulltime professional gambler, which he found a much more congenial pursuit.

After the killer of several men had joined the table, Watts jestingly advised him, "Ben, you will be took off sudden one of these days and I may not be around to sell a tombstone to ornament your grave. You had better order one from me now."

The gunman replied, "A wooden board is about all I need," and he continued to gamble, eventually wiping out all the cash that Watts had brought to town. When the peddler started to get up from the table, Thompson stopped him, having had second thoughts about the idea of getting a grave marker in advance of its need.

"Hold on there," he asked. "How much are them tombstones of yours worth?" Watts replied that the cost depended on the stone, saying that he had a fine piece of marble in his wagon that would make a beautiful marker. The stone was worth two hundred dollars, "which is cheap," he added, "considering that it is a long ways from the quarries." Thomas then declared, "Put that tombstone in the pot against my $200 and I will play with you win or lose," and asked the salesman to get the marble slab so that everyone could examine it.

By this time it was two o'clock in the morning, but Watts proceeded back to the wagon yard, hitched up his team, and delivered the stone to the front of the saloon. Porters helped haul it upstairs to the gaming rooms and sat it down beside Thompson, who said that he was satisfied with it.

It only took a few more minutes for the game to wind down, the gunman winning the proceeds, but Watts seemed unconcerned about the outcome. "Better let me carve the inscription on it now," he said, but Thompson declined. "No, you can wait until I have done something that will give you the subject for a befitting epitaph," he said.

For the next few days the stone lay in the gaming rooms, and then the saloon owner had it carried downstairs, where no one thought very much about it. Then, years later, when the saloon building was demolished, workmen discovered the long forgotten monument.

As for Ben Thompson, he was killed in a shooting at the Vaudeville Theater in San Antonio in March 1884. He was brought back to Austin and buried in an unmarked grave. No one remembered that his tombstone was waiting for him at the Iron Front Saloon.

The Headless Horseman of the Nueces

For weeks during the fall of 1850, reports had circulated in the Nueces River country about sightings of a headless horseman mounted astride a magnificent black mustang. No one had approached the seeming apparition close enough to inspect it until a party of frontiersmen succeeded in shooting the horse in order to satisfy their curiosities about what it was carrying.

What did they find?

Tied with ropes and thongs to the saddle were the remains of a small, dried-up Mexican man, his head bound into a sombrero and tied to the saddle horn. The almost mummified corpse was perforated with rifle balls, evidently fired by others who had thought that they were shooting at a ghost.

How did the headless man end up tied to the horse?

The story goes back to the summer preceding, when a party of horse thieves headed by a man called Vidal raided the area around San Antonio unmercifully. A former deserter from Mexican troops who aided the Texan insurgents during the Texas Revolution, Vidal in the subsequent years came to head a ring of professional horse thieves that ranged from Nacogdoches to the interior of Mexico. They often left Indian signs at the scenes of their depredations to divert attention from themselves.

In summer 1850, Vidal and a party of his men made a particular raid into the valley of the San Antonio River. The foray took place just after another one by the Comanche Indians into the Cibolo Creek and

Guadalupe River valleys, so most of the able-bodied men were away from the settlements attempting to punish the thieves.

Having taken all the horses that he and his three companions could handle, Vidal headed westward toward the Rio Grande. Unknown to the thieves, they were being followed by frontiersman Creed Taylor and one of his neighbors, a rancher named Flores. As the two followed the trail of the stolen stock, they met Bigfoot Wallace, who also had a grievance with Vidal over thievery.

The three ranchers pushed onward, fatiguing themselves and their mounts, until they came up on Vidal and his confederates in camp on the Nueces about twelve miles below Fort Inge in present-day Uvalde County. They found the rustlers near the river in an open area with knee-high grass. "We were somewhat surprised to see those fellows go into camp," Creed Taylor later stated, "as we expected them to continue on the run through the night."

The ranchers, each armed with a Colt revolver and a rifle, left the rustlers in peace until about eleven o'clock that night. Then they sneaked up on the thieves in the darkness, Flores creeping up to the one sentry at the horse herd, while Taylor and Wallace made their way through the tall grass to the camp proper.

As a pre-arranged signal, Flores shot the sentry with his rifle. "The three sleepers sprang to their feet, and on the same instant our rifles blazed," Taylor remembered. "The scrimmage was all over in a minute." Only the sentry escaped, his blood on the grass marking a trail that the ranchers didn't bother to follow.

When daylight broke, the three settlers examined the bodies of the thieves. "Our gratification was indeed great when we identified the body of the small Mexican as being that of Vidal." Taylor declared.

Although there was a reward for the capture of the outlaw, the frontiersmen decided that they would forego the reward in order to make an example of him. Bigfoot Wallace provided the plan. "At his suggestion," Taylor remembered, "we roped a fine large mustang, the wildest in the herd, threw him down, and selected the strongest saddle from among the spoils." They then secured the saddle to the animal.

Continuing the grim proceedings, "He cut off Vidal's head [and] mounted the headless trunk in a natural upright position in the saddle, where we fastened it securely with ropes and thongs taken from the other captured saddles." Were this not enough already, Taylor continued, "We next bound his hat firmly on his head and hung it, his head, to the horn of the saddle by passing the pommel string through the hat strap that passed under the wearer's jaws and chin."

Their work completed, Creed Taylor described the finished job: "He presented the appearance of a horseman, who, instead of wearing his head where it ought to be worn, had it slung to the horn of his saddle and allowed it to rest against his thigh."

In this state, the three ranchers released the mustang, which seemed to realize the nature of its burden and did everything to buck and shake it off. "When he found that he couldn't get rid of his uncanny rider," Creed Taylor related, "he broke away with accelerating speed, and when we saw him last he looked like a vanishing speck on the distant horizon."

An Army Scout's Memories of Home

John Woodland, an English-born scout for the army at Fort Inge, Texas, certainly knew how to take care of himself in tight places. He survived numerous fights that few people could even imagine.

Connecticut Yankee Frederick Law Olmstead met Woodland at the garrison in present-day Uvalde County in the mid-1850s, as he traveled through the state gathering material for a book on life in Texas. Woodland guided him to the Rio Grande country, and during their days together on horseback, the two men became well acquainted.

Olmstead liked Woodland, whom he found "neat, quiet and orderly." He wrote specifically that his guide was "communicative without being garrulous and tiresome," a quality that he found in no other Texas frontiersman.

A native of England, the scout initially asserted that he had no memories of home. He had immigrated with his family as a young lad to Ohio, where he had gone to school, ending up in a company of volunteer soldiers that fought in the 1846 Mexican War. While in the military, the immigrant learned to speak fluent Spanish so well, according to Olmstead, that "he could assume the Mexican manner and tongue so perfectly that the Mexicans would not believe that he had not been born in their country."

On one occasion during the war in Mexico, Woodland's unit inadvertently intercepted a much greater force of Mexican troops. Not knowing what else to do, they decided to charge pell-mell through the ranks of the enemy, each man looking out for himself. Woodland survived the affray, but only after suffering a blow which left his right arm nearly powerless for the rest of his days.

After the war the Englishman found employment as a civilian scout for the army and as a guide and interpreter for travelers doing business in Mexico. Thus it was that Olmstead sought him out when he reached Fort Inge on the way to the border country.

One day as Woodland and Olmstead were riding along, the scout asked his client, who had traveled in Britain, "Aren't there little flowers that grow along by the fence in England that they call cups?"

"Yes," Olmstead answered. "Buttercups."

"And another little flower in the fences that smell very nice—haws, is it?" he asked.

"Primroses," Olmstead suggested.

"Ah, yes, that's it—cups and primroses."

Thinking back about his earliest memories of childhood, the hardened survivor of the Southwestern frontier softened as he shared with the traveler: "I can remember going out with my mother into the country and picking them. That's the only thing I can remember in England."

Impressions of "King" Fisher

J. K. "King" Fisher was one of the most noted of the Texas gunmen in the lawless years following the Civil War. A native of Kentucky, he came to Texas at age thirteen with his father, who shortly thereafter died from wounds he received in an affray with federal troops near Fort Worth.

Fisher became a cowboy who in time drifted into rustling as a livelihood. Much of his income reputedly came from fencing property for Texans whose horses and cattle had been stolen in Mexico.

Vinton L. James was a sheepherder in Uvalde County, where Fisher operated in the early 1880s, and he was impressed with "King's" skill in roping and breaking wild horses. "His work in the pen was wonderful," he reported. "He would toss the lariat among a bunch of running horses and catch the wanted one, sometimes by the head, and often by roping the running animal's two front feet." This would throw the horse to the ground, and before it could rise, "King" was on it and had it tied down.

James remembered Fisher as being "not a large man" but rather "sparely built, with a handsome face," his movements "rapid and graceful." Fisher proposed joining James in the ranching business; James would continue to handle the sheep and Fisher would buy and sell horses. But James hesitated to accept the offer because of Fisher's reputation for violence. On one occasion a grand jury considered charges of eleven murders by Fisher, but returned no indictments because there were no bodies.

Jane Maverick with her husband, Albert, lived on a Bandera County ranch and she remembered one night that "King" Fisher came for supper. "He arrived late one evening with a lot of cowboys and a good sized bunch of cattle," she said. He asked if his men and animals could spend the night, and the Mavericks could hardly refuse the request.

"Someone explained that he wished to sleep in the house for fear of being killed in the night by some of his various enemies," Mrs. Maverick related. On account of his dealings, Fisher had a multitude of adversaries. He was so notorious in South Texas that on one occasion he erected a sign on a branch road that read: "This is King Fisher's road. Take the other." It was unusual for anyone to disregard the advice.

When Mrs. Maverick served dinner for her guest together with her family, Fisher was careful to sit where he would not present a target for a gunman outdoors. Even so he was visibly nervous. When Rose Kalka, a Polish servant girl in the house, happened to touch him in serving the meal to the table, Jane Maverick recalled, "he jumped like his time had come."

Overnight Fisher retired to a small room built onto the porch of the house, but Jane Maverick slept very little. "After all was quiet," she stated, "I spent a very restless time—and one time when he got up to get a drink of water from the bucket, I held my baby very tight thinking we would die together."

When morning finally came, Fisher, his men, and his cattle proceeded on their journey, and Jane Maverick breathed a sigh of relief. Not very long thereafter, on March 11, 1884, "King" Fisher and his friend, gunman Ben Thompson, were both killed by unknown assailants in a San Antonio saloon. Jane Maverick declared, "I hope [he] passed on to the happy hunting ground."

IV.

PANHANDLE PLAINS

Blasting the Heavens for Rain

Almost 125 years ago this August the C Ranch in Andrews County, Texas, witnessed an amazing event—the largest scale rainmaking experiment ever conducted in the United States up to that date. It was a sight to behold.

The story of the rainmakers actually goes back to the ancient Greek historian, Plutarch, who first observed that rain usually followed great battles. His theory was based on divine intervention coupled with the effects of blood and putrefaction on the atmosphere, but a century ago scientists applied his thoughts to the battles of their day, which were accompanied by incredible discharges of gunpowder. Veterans of the Civil War at the time encouraged belief in the theory on account of the many muddy campaigns they had experienced.

After considerable political pressure, the U.S. Congress in 1890 appropriated two thousand dollars to fund a series of officially sanctioned experiments by the Department of Agriculture to ascertain whether mass explosions of gunpowder did indeed cause rainfall. Assisted by donations of transportation and explosive chemicals from railways and chemical firms, the members of the rainmaking expedition headed by Robert St. George Dryenforth gathered on the C Ranch about a day's ride northwest of Midland in late July 1891.

The experimenters tested the theory that explosive concussions caused rain by breaking a presumed balanced state of nature that would then allow natural processes to begin creating rain clouds. The more concussions they could make, the more out of balance they would throw the equilibrium to prompt precipitation.

The scientists and their cowboy helpers made their concussions by firing charges from makeshift cannons fashioned from well casing and hollow iron wagon axles, by blowing up sticks of dynamite sent aloft in large kites, and by igniting mixed hydrogen and oxygen sent into the heavens inside ten foot-wide varnished cloth balloons.

A reporter from *Farm Implement News* on the scene at the time noted for his readers, "large quantities of dynamite, 'rackarock' blasting powder, and oxy-hydrogen gas were exploded, partly on the ground and partly at heights ranging from a few feet to a mile and a half, the explosives being hung from mesquite brush and poles, suspended from large kites, or contained in balloons and exploded by means of electricity or with time fuses or dynamite caps." It's a wonder that no one was killed.

Although there were a few rain showers at and around the site of the experiments on the Texas plains, none of them appeared to have come as a consequence of the concussive explosions. The farm implement magazine reporter observed critically, "It is probably true that more atmospheric concussion was made by the jackrabbit hunters in the vicinity in one day than was caused by the combined efforts of the rainmakers." The results of the month of explosions that rocked the C Ranch headquarters were debatable at best.

Head rainmaker Robert Dryenforth, however, claimed responsibility for all the showers that chanced to fall in the region. On the conclusion of his Andrews County experiments at the end of August 1891, he hastened to Washington to solicit more Congressional funds and tell reporters of his purported success. The lack of actual concussion-caused rain certainly didn't dampen the spirits of the rainmakers, and they continued their unsuccessful efforts to blast rain out of the heavens.

Watching the Death of the Buffalo

In the Texas Panhandle in 1876, Adolph Hunnius repeatedly wrote in his diary of seeing "hundreds and hundreds of buffalo, sometimes in front and sometimes on both sides." The year 1876, however, was the last that the shaggies were seen in such numbers.

Hunnius was the draftsman for a U.S. Army Engineers topographic surveying expedition that mapped the central Panhandle during the spring and summer of 1876. The army surveyors saw some of the last big herds of buffalo in the Panhandle. Expedition commander Lieutenant Ernest Howard Ruffner later remembered, "We were soon in the buffalo, but instead of the countless herds of five years before, the bands were small and not numerous. Thousands ran where tens of thousands were found in 1872."

The cause for the declining herds was the activity of professional buffalo hunters. Starting in 1872 they had begun slaughtering the bison for their skins, which were processed into leather on the East Coast and in Europe. Lieutenant Ruffner described seeing the hunters "hanging on the flanks of the herd," but he added that their destructive work had already been so thorough that "the pursuit is not very remunerative, and I doubt if any who were out made much more than a fair living by their campaign."

The army surveyors did not kill the animals for their skins, but they did shoot several buffaloes for meat. On May 16, 1876, Adolph Hunnius recorded in his diary, "We saw 6 buffaloes and after a while I proposed to Teodoso to make a chase. . . . And we went. We singled out a young looking bull and after a sharp chase we succeeded in turning him off. Teodoso brought him down. . . . The corporal gave him two shots, and I had no show at all."

Hunnius went on to describe the butchering process: "We took all good meat, as hindquarters and forequarters, tenderloins, liver and tongue. Out a wagon came over from the train [to haul the meat]. We washed our hands with water out of the canteens and at 8:30 we were moving again."

A month later the draftsman commented on the pages of his diary, "We had several opportunities to shoot at buffalo, but as the train [of wagons] was too far away from us and there would be no chance to transport the meat, I could not see why to waste ammunition."

Although he participated in killing bison for camp meat supply, draftsman Hunnius was revolted by the carnage left behind by the hide hunters. On June 20, 1876, he wrote in his journal: "A mile from our camp we passed over a great many places where the buffalo hunters had made a stand and killed the animals up to 25 in a small place. The stench of the carcasses was awful. The hunters cut the heads off to turn better the bodies."

Lieutenant Ruffner summed up things succinctly when he wrote, "The buffalo have no longer here a home."

Eating on a Government Survey

"I had a small slice of fat bacon and tomatoes and a cup of coffee, which is rather not much till tomorrow." Adolph Hunnius wrote these words in his diary for April 29, 1876. He was right. It was a lousy meal.

Adolph Hunnius was a civilian draftsman who accompanied a U.S. Army Engineers group surveying the headwaters of the Red River in the Texas Panhandle during the spring and summer of 1876. The purpose of the expedition was to prepare detailed maps of the upper reaches of the Red River for use in any future military operations in the area.

The survey party traveled by train from Fort Leavenworth to Dodge City, Kansas, and then continued by wagon from there via Camp Supply in Oklahoma to Fort Elliott, in the extreme eastern Texas Panhandle. Fort Elliott, where the actual survey began, had been founded the year before and was the only permanent U.S. Army fort in the Panhandle.

Throughout the survey, German-born draftsman Hunnius kept detailed notes in his diary, now preserved at the University of Kansas. On May 3, 1876, the first day out of Camp Supply, he recorded that he "had a very good dinner prepared by Mr. Sullivan: Fried ham, green corn, good coffee and milk." Sullivan was one of the civilian teamsters with whom Hunnius ate. There were two additional messes in the expedition, one for the officers and the other for the enlisted men composing a military escort.

Various foods found along the route ended up in the frying pans of the surveyors. On May 14 Hunnius wrote that "McClellan Creek has rather dirty looking water, but a great many catfish are in it and Mr. Sullivan caught many, some very big ones." The next day he added, "Reveille at 4 this morning. Had fish for breakfast."

Buffalo meat became a staple item in the surveyors' diet during much of their time in the field. On May 31, "for dinner Mr. Sullivan had buffalo meat chopped and some bacon fried with it. It was a splendid meal," Hunnius noted.

Some of the meals were real treats. On May 15, for instance, Hunnius commented "for supper we had coffee and jelly cake, which

Mr. Sullivan made to the great astonishment of all who saw it. It tasted very fine and was surely a surprize."

A few of the meals ended up being real disappointments. Ruefully the German penned on May 17, "We expected to have such a nice breakfast of stewed buffalo meat. Mr. Sullivan had put it last night in a covered pan and put it in a hole surrounded by hot coals, and covered it up with ground. During the night someone must have stepped on the handle, because it was half upset and pretty well spoiled by sand and ashes having fallen in."

Cooking utensils were limited on military survey expeditions. The draftsman wrote in his diary for May 25, "As I do not know much of cooking, do the washing of our 'Mess Kit' [consisting of] 2 tin plates, 2 tin cups, 2 knives and forks, and one spoon. The big frying pan has to answer as the article to wash the dishes in. Well, out here anything will do."

Finally, toward the close of the survey on June 4, 1876, Hunnius awakened to a damp, 48 degree, cold morning, and wrote in his diary a memo with which most of us today can readily identify: "Warm coffee was quite the thing."

Roadrunners and Magpies

Roadrunners can be seen just about anywhere in Texas from Nacogdoches to El Paso, from Amarillo to Del Rio. They're probably second in popularity among Texans only to our own state bird, the mockingbird.

The lightning-fast runners always intrigue newcomers when they first encounter them, and it was no different aver a century ago.

Back in the spring and summer of 1876, Lieutenant Charles A. H. McCauley participated in a scientific expedition for the U.S. Army that surveyed and mapped the area of the headwaters of the Red River in the Panhandle. Among his duties was collecting specimens of all the birds observed by the party. One of these species was the roadrunner.

In his subsequent report he discussed its similarity to the magpie—an unexpected likeness.

The appearance of the roadrunner was the first thing to attract McCauley's attention. An "odd-looking bird," he noted, recording its long neck and beak and its muscular legs. These legs gave the bird its greatest protection in its preferred brushy environment. McCauley wrote, "He travels only on foot, and the celerity of his movements in such a mass of tangle-brush is wonderful."

The roadrunner's cry is distinctive if not pleasant. McCauley described it as "a succession of low chuckles, grating harshly at first, softening at the end, and repeated often if you get near a pair. A few of the notes bring to mind the call of a barnyard cock to his hen . . . once heard and fairly caught, you will always remember it."

The lieutenant discovered curiosity to be one of the most prominent characteristics of the roadrunner. "He never fails to gratify it. If there is any unfamiliar sound over the ridge above him, up comes his head over the top, and he stops for a moment to stare. That suffices, however, and if the object be strange and apparently unfriendly or in pursuit, he is off like a flash."

Lieutenant McCauley had a friend who for a number of years lived at Brownsville in the Lower Rio Grande Valley. This friend told him of another trait common to the roadrunners.

Residents in the lower valley sometimes captured baby roadrunners from their nests and raised them at home as pets. The tamed birds exhibited a characteristic for which magpies are better known—an overwhelming compulsion to eat shiny objects. The officer wrote, "For bright buttons, or anything of brass or glittering, they have an insatiable craving."

In one instance at Brownsville, a local belle had a roadrunner as a household pet. It had a free range of the home, going wherever it wished in and out of the doors and windows. On one occasion, however, the pet spied its mistress's pride and joy, a glistening brooch. The bird "got his eye on a breast-pin," McCauley wrote, "and promptly went for it, and bolted it whole."

The brooch didn't stay too long in the roadrunner's craw, for his pretty owner's love of jewelry overcame her fondness for the bird, "and the pet was sacrificed."

It's Blabbing Time

Winter is the season for "blabbing." About this time of the year, the mother cows begin to suffer from the poor grazing, but their maturing calves still insist on nursing. This greed of the calves deprives their mothers of usable sustenance. I'd always called the taking of the calves from their mothers as "weaning," but then I learned about "blabbing" when I read *Life on a Ranch* written by Reginald Aldridge back in 1884.

Aldridge had come to America in 1878 from England, seeking his fortune on the giant cattle ranches of the Great Plains. He first settled in southwestern Kansas, but before long he relocated near Mobeetie in the Texas Panhandle.

While residing in Texas, Aldridge wrote *Life on a Ranch* to advise his fellow countrymen back in England about what they might expect if they invested in American ranches. At the time there was a craze in England for investing in western livestock operations.

"One of our occupations as winter advanced," Aldridge wrote for his readers at home, "consisted of 'blabbing' calves." He went on to explain that this weaning took place in the wintertime when the mother cows began growing thin.

Next he described the "blab" itself. This, he explained, was a light piece of wooden board about four by six inches "shaped so that you can just force it onto the membrane that divides the nostrils of a calf." With the blab in place, the calf could easily graze on grass but could not suck from its mother.

"When you start out on a blabbing expedition," Aldridge advised, "you place several blabs in your pocket and ride along till you see a big calf whose dam looks as if she would be better for being relieved of the support of her progeny."

The next step was to rope the calf, which might be easy if you'd done it all your life, but which was less than simple for Englishman Aldridge. He described Texan calf roping for his readers this way: "You take your lariat off your saddle, and, holding it in convenient coils in your left hand, with the running noose in your right, you gallop after the calf till you get close to it." He continued, "Then you whirl the noose round your head two or three times to get a good swing, and launch it at the head of the calf."

Awkward on horseback at best, the Englishman commented, "If you are like me, you will probably find no result, the calf continuing to pursue his way across the prairie with the same vigor as before." Aldridge then advised that if one had "a professional cow-boy" along, then the expert could proceed and rope the recalcitrant animal.

Actual blabbing, once the calf was captured, was comparatively simple. "When you have the calf roped it is an easy matter to throw him down and stick the blab on his nose, after which you turn him loose and go in quest of another."

Mother to the Whole Cow Country

"Mother to the whole cow country" is the way that Mrs. Mose Hays was remembered, and it was a title she deserved.

In 1881 Mose Hays and his new bride, described as "a stocky, black-eyed girl," came to Springer's Ranch. The place was both a cattle ranch and a "road ranch" or store on the old military road from Dodge City, Kansas, southward to Fort Elliott, in the eastern Texas Panhandle. The ranch centered at the point where Boggy Creek flowed southward into the Canadian River just west of the line between Texas and the Indian Territory.

The ranch had been established by A. G. "Jim" Springer in 1874 or 1875, and had passed through several owners. When Mr. and Mrs. Hays arrived to manage the place, it belonged to the Rhodes and Aldridge Cattle Company. Eventually Hays purchased the enterprise.

Springer's Ranch became a home, for wherever Mrs. Hays lived was a home. Panhandle historian Laura V. Hamner wrote of her: "She mended the clothes of the cowboys, washing and carefully laying away any discarded garment, so that it might serve as patches for the worn shirt or trousers of some other boy in distress."

Throughout the region people knew of Mrs. Hays's cooking. Hamner continued, "She cooked for the boys, nursed them in illness, sent them a cake when they were off in camp and made berry cobblers in the largest container on the place to take to roundups." Oliver Nelson, at the time one of the cowboys on the Canadian, later recalled that whenever a cowpoke was in the vicinity, he would drop in at Mose Hays's place for dinner "and get acquainted with the missus."

Before long the transients were eating more food than Mose and his wife could afford to buy, but Mrs. Hays reputedly told her husband, "We'll fight it through, and do it free." Realizing the effects of their freeloading, the cowboys began hauling in beef, flour, sugar, and coffee, more even than was needed. "At Christmas they brought several turkeys and everyone went to Mose's cabin for a big time," Nelson reminisced.

The following spring the cowboys registered a brand in Mrs. Hays's name and used it to mark all the maverick calves they came across. When the roundup later took place, she discovered that she was the owner of 250 head of cattle.

Mrs. Hays was more than just a good cook. Laura Hamner wrote, "She did all that a loving mother would do, but perhaps her greatest contribution to a world where men were so much alone that they forgot how to laugh was to bring back their laughter. She teased them, told jokes, gave a lilt to life. She always knew a boy the next time she saw him, no matter how slight the acquaintance, a rare virtue in the eyes of lonely, bashful boys."

In the late 1880s, Mose Hays and his wife in failing health left Springer's Ranch, settling on Commission Creek, the next creek to the north, where sub irrigated land gave good pasturage and created a little lake known as Bonnie Hays Lake. There their little girl played within the sight of her dying mother.

Still the cowboys came to see Mrs. Hays, bringing with them their sweethearts, wives and babies, and sharing with her their joys and sorrows.

To the very last she smiled.

Human or Buffalo Bones on the Canadian

When you visit Adobe Walls, there's not too much to see, but on the brown ground around what used to be the Myers and Leonard store white flecks appear. Upon closer inspection, they appear to be flakes of animal bone . . . but—again—are they?

Adobe Walls was a trading post begun by Dodge City merchants in March 1874. On the north bank of the Canadian River in present-day Hutchinson County, Texas, it served crews of Kansas buffalo hide hunters and skinners who had shifted their operations southward into the Panhandle the preceding winter. There they bought their supplies and sold their raw hides.

The post consisted of four business enterprises: the Myers and Leonard store, Tom O'Keefe's blacksmith shop, Jim Hanrahan's saloon, and the Rath and Company store. Both of the stores competed in the restaurant trade as well as in selling general merchandise, and buffalo roast, tongue, and steak together with the remainder of the meals sold briskly at an average price of a dollar a day for board. Lots of bones from the butchered meat resulted.

Life for the handful of traders and their customers changed dramatically on June 27, 1874. Before dawn two hundred Comanche, Kiowa, and Comanche warriors descended on the post. A laborer in the Rath store later remembered, "It was a case of every fellow for himself and 'get' as many Indians as possible."

At the end of the day, three whites lay victims of the attackers, while thirteen Indians had fallen so close to the stores that their comrades could not retrieve their bodies.

The Battle of Adobe Walls had been a standoff.

The defenders buried their dead wrapped in a blanket in a single grave. They decided to wait until hunters came in from outlying camps to help in drawing away the dead draft animals and Indian corpses, which already were beginning to decompose.

When the other hunters came in, they had different ideas. The hardened frontiersmen cut off the heads of each of the fallen warriors so they could use them to decorate the gate leading into the hide yard at the Myers and Leonard store. Each head was stuck on a wooden peg.

W. C. Cox, one of the participants in the grim proceedings, later remembered, "We pitched out their headless bodies like you would a dead dog's." Another of the hide men, "Brick" Bond, noting how the skin drew away from the eyes and mouths as it dried, declared, "They looked like they had been laughing when their heads were cut off."

The warriors' bones remained there, readily recognized by visitors for decades. But today they are weathered away to white flecks on the brown ground, mixed with those from the buffalo that were butchered for the two restaurants.

When you look down on the white fragments on the brown earth at Adobe Walls, look closely. Can you tell? Do they come from humans of times past or from buffalo?

The Sacred Comanche Medicine Stone

"I made them some presents and obtained from them a promise to show me this extraordinary piece of metal," wrote Anthony Glass in his journal for September 19, 1809.

Glass was heading an Anglo-American trading expedition from Louisiana among the Taovaya Indians on the Red River. Just a few days before he had heard of "a remarkable piece of metal some days distant to the southward on the waters of the River Brassos." The "metal" in question was a meteorite—a very extraordinary meteorite.

Anthony Glass, thinking that the object might be platinum or some other precious metal, succeeded in convincing his Indian hosts with gifts of trade goods to lead him to the sacred stone. They took him to a camp of Comanche Indians, known to him as "Hietans," on the west Fork of the Trinity. "We found about twenty tents," he noted in his journal for October 7. "They are made of different sizes of buffalo skins and supported on poles made from red cedar." In order to make a favorable impression, "I presented the Hietan chief with some blankets and trinkets."

Glass continued his story, "They made some objections to showing it [the meteorite], and I was obliged to flatter and bribe him to go on." After passing through some broken country and crossing the Brazos, they approached the locality of the sacred medicine stone. The area has been identified by Texas Tech historian Dan L. Flores as having been in the eastern part of present-day Shackelford County, Texas.

As the Indians neared the sacred place, Glass commented that they observed "considerable ceremony." On his arrival at the site, the trader found the meteorite "resting on its heaviest end and leaning toward one side." Beneath it were some tobacco pipes and other ceremonial objects "placed there by some Indians who had been healed by visiting it." The actual medicine stone, a very dense cone-shaped heavy object, measured roughly 40 x 24 x 16 inches. "It had the color of iron, but no rust upon it." Glass observed, "There is no reason to think it had ever been moved by men."

After knocking off some small pieces of the metallic stone to take home to Louisiana, Glass left the sacred Comanche medicine stone and continued his trading expedition. No sooner had he returned to Natchitoches, Louisiana, however, than did two more groups of men start planning to set out for the Comanche country in order to retrieve the medicine stone. They were convinced that the object was composed of some precious metal that they could sell.

In June 1809 a party of Americans headed by George Schamp and Ezra McCall, funded by American Indian agent John Sibley, left for the plains from Natchitoches. About the same time another group of frontiersmen headed by John Davis departed Natchez, Mississippi, for western Texas. The two rival groups both were after the medicine stone.

Thomas M. Dade, a member of the Schamp-McCall party, related that a member of the Glass expedition had reported about the stone, "The Comanches regarded it as sacred and even worshiped it," to which Dade added, "A god of platinum seemed worth *our* homage too, and we were determined to brave almost any danger to obtain it."

While the Schamp-McCall party negotiated with the Taovaya Indians on the Red River to trade for the stone, the Davis expedition went straight to the site and simply took it without the permission of any of the tribes. Because the meteorite was so heavy, over 1,500 pounds, they could only roll it away and hide it beneath some rocks.

In the meantime, the Schamp-McCall party arrived on the scene and perplexingly discovered the stone missing. Soon a member of the group located it. They then manhandled the meteorite into a horse-drawn cart and started a long, tedious journey back to Natchitoches by way of the Red River. Part of the way they even floated the stone downstream on the river in a hollowed-out black walnut tree.

When the Comanche medicine stone finally reached Natchitoches, Indian agent John Sibley shipped it on to New York City for analysis. There, to the disappointment of all, it was found to be composed of an iron-nickel mixture and to contain no precious metals. The men who had risked their lives in going to the Comanche country to bring back the sacred stone, however, never gave up their belief that it was valuable. They were correct that it was valuable—but not for any platinum that it might contain. Its value was scientific.

The sacred Comanche medicine stone found its way to the Peabody Museum of Natural History at Yale University, where it became internationally known as the largest meteorite collected up to its day. Now superseded by larger meteorites located elsewhere in the world, it is still the largest meteorite ever found in Texas.

The Grave of Zemula Metcalfe

Teenaged Zemula Metcalfe lies in the Ben Ficklin Cemetery because of her mother's stubbornness.

The graveyard is scattered across a rocky knoll overlooking the busy freeway intersection of U.S. Highways 87 and 277 on the south side of present-day San Angelo. Other than a few historical markers, this little used cemetery is all that remains of the once booming town of Ben Ficklin.

Established in 1871, Ben Ficklin became the seat of Tom Green County when it was organized in 1875. Although the town experienced some commercial competition from the saloon town of Santa Angela (now San Angelo), four miles away and adjacent to the military garrison at Fort Concho, Ben Ficklin remained the commercial center for the county, even boasting of its own fine two-story stone courthouse.

All this changed, however, on Thursday, August 24, 1882. After a very wet summer, the waters of the forks of the Concho River and their tributaries began rising on that morning after additional heavy rains, and by the middle of the day the flood was washing away the last remnants of Ben Ficklin. Sixty people lost their lives, among them pretty Zemula Metcalfe.

Mrs. M. J. Metcalfe, Zemula's mother, and her family of five with their Black cook were at the stagecoach station just south of Ben Ficklin on the morning of August 24. They had watched the floodwaters come into their home, and they retreated to the stage station, which was on somewhat higher ground. Mr. C. D. Foote realized that the people at the station might become trapped if the water continued to rise, and he carried away several of them in his wagon.

Zemula's mother, however, said that she thought that the flood had already reached its crest. One of her sons, Charles, a survivor of the flood, later wrote, "My mother could also have left, but she was perfectly fearless and did not believe there was great danger," so the Metcalfes remained at the station. When Foote asked Zemula if she would like to retreat to higher ground, she replied, "My place is with mother," and she stayed.

As the waters continued to rise, Mr. S. C. Robertson of Santa Angela, who also had remained at the stage station, became convinced it was time to retreat. In a horse-drawn hack he successfully drove his wife to safety on higher ground.

Robertson next bravely drove back to the stage station, each minute deeper in the water, to carry away the people still there, whom he loaded into his vehicle. The contemporary press reported, "They started, but the horses balked, and no progress was possible." Robertson had really managed to get into a fix. "At Mrs. Metcalfe's suggestion they turned, and by means of a ladder, climbed upon the roof of her dwelling." There they all sat stranded, the waters still rising.

Son Charles Metcalfe described the next minutes: "While the four persons with my mother were on the housetop at the mail station, about ten o'clock, a most heroic attempt of rescue was made by Terrell Harris and Kirby Smith, a blacksmith." Using a "boat" hastily made by nailing boards together, the two men, one white and the other black, set out to save the stranded Metcalfe family members, their cook, S. C. Robertson, and a Mexican known as Anselmo, all of them caught on the roof.

Metcalfe continued the narrative: "They . . . launched themselves into the fearful torrent. It was impossible to steer or row the boat, which was tossed like a feather in the wind, for the mile of distance downstream where they were swept to within a few feet of the party on the roof, whom they were unable, however, to save." Four hundred yards farther downstream the boat was upset and tossed the two rescuers themselves into the waters, from which they eventually were saved.

The group on the roof was not so fortunate. "Nearly at the same time" as the capsizing of the erstwhile rescuers' boat, according to the press, "the roof with its living freight broke in two, the ladies clinging to one half and the men to the other."

The men lost their holds on their part of the roof and were swept into the raging waters. "The ladies," the press reported, "bore down upon the pecan clump and were engulphed." The sole survivor from the party on the roof was S. C. Robertson, the man who had come back to the stage station after saving his wife to help the stranded people there to get away. The local press reported, "Mr. S. C. Robertson was shaken from the roof, but caught a tree and held on through as terrible a day and night as anyone ever endured."

The deluge destroyed the hopes of Ben Ficklin, which never was rebuilt, leaving behind only its cemetery with the grave of Zemula Metcalfe while at the same time the flood insured the success of its commercial rival, San Angelo, which now booms just a short distance away.

Three Boys in the Same Grave

I found all three of them there just like I'd heard—three boys killed by the Indians at Proffitt in 1867. Their grave stands at the back of the little country cemetery on U.S. 380 about eight miles west of Newcastle in Young County. They were the first ones there. They started the graveyard.

Now they are all but forgotten by everyone accept for a handful of local residents and maybe a few historians like me. A crudely laid red brick wall surrounds the burial, and a tree grows up inside of it. At one side some iris plants rustle in the West Texas breeze. It's almost always peaceful there.

How did the three boys end up in the grave together?

The story goes back to the summer of 1867, when they were tending cattle on Elm Creek, then on the fringe of white settlement. They were Patrick Euell Proffitt, Rice Oarlton, and Reuben Johnson, all of them teenagers. They were working as cowboys on the FitzPatrick Ranch.

On July 17, 1867, the three boys went to work branding cattle in the valley of Elm Creek. The area had been the scene of a devastating Indian raid only three years before. Maybe they felt safe from attack, thinking that the warriors wouldn't descend on the same valley a second time. Whatever the case, they unwisely left their guns on their saddles and allowed their horses to graze while they worked.

Without warning a Comanche war party rode into view. The three boys made for their horses—and their firearms—but they weren't lucky enough to reach them. The Comanches cut them off from their guns and horses. Without defense, the three young men were shot down by the warriors, who scalped them and left them where they fell.

Local settlers buried the three boys near the place where they were attacked, placing all three of them in the same grave. Their burial became the site for other graves in the years that followed, becoming the cemetery for what grew into the town of Proffitt.

The nearby town bearing the same name as one of the ill-fated teenagers was founded by the dead man's brother, John W. Proffitt. It prospered for a number of years before declining to become a scattered rural community.

Since the deaths of the three young men, descendants of their families and members of the local community have tended their grave. In 1966 historically minded citizens of Young County placed a new marker at the grave, which briefly tells the story of the three deaths.

When I opened the gate to the cyclone fence into the Proffitt Cemetery to look for the victims of the Indians that I'd heard were buried there, I didn't know what to expect as I wandered among the tombstones. Then, when I found the low brick wall around the burial, somehow my mind went back to that hot day in July 1867—the sorrow of the families, the desire for revenge, and the blood from the three boys that still nourishes the tree that grows from their grave.

V.

PINEY WOODS

A Texas Town Sold for Scrap

M. B. Tyre of Lufkin bought the entire town of Manning—bought it so that he could have the buildings torn down and their materials sold in Dallas, Houston, and Lufkin. This was back in 1937, but the story of the town begins much earlier.

For 120 years Manning has witnessed on-again, off-again lumbering activity. Located in the Neches Valley of Angelina County roughly ten miles south of Huntington, its vicinity today is meadow-like green pasture. When Manning was born, however, it was mostly covered with East Texas pines. These trees were the reason for the town.

Back in 1867 Dr. W. W. Manning established a sawmill near the site that later became the town. For a few years the mill sawed lumber from pines cut in the Neches bottoms, but then it fell silent. Renewed lumbering activity began in 1906, when the Carter-Kelley Lumber Company built a large mill to process timber from the surrounding forests. It was no small operation, for the mill soon was producing thirty-four million board feet of lumber annually and employing three hundred men.

Serving the town that grew up beside the mill, the Shreveport, Houston, and Gulf Railroad built south from Huntington to connect the mill with the main line of the Southern Pacific and Cotton Belt. Since its initials were S. H. and G., the local residents jokingly called it the "Shove Hard and Grunt" line.

Manning grew to become a very substantial town with an estimated 1,600 people. In its heyday it had not only lodge halls, theaters, a hotel, elementary and high schools, and hundreds of residences, but also a huge, rambling company-owned general mercantile store that reputedly sold everything from nails to caskets. Residents named the main street "Dirty Street." Like all the others in the town, it was unpaved. It was muddy almost all the time in the often rainy East Texas climate.

The end for Manning came very quickly. In January 1935 an uncontrolled fire swept through the sawmill complex, leaving only its concrete foundations behind. Economic difficulties during the Great Depression coupled with the depleted state of local timber reserves prompted the company to abandon the mill completely. Over the next few months, most of the former employees drifted away to other jobs, leaving just a handful to begin farming.

Then in 1937 M. B. Tyre entered the picture. When company officials announced that they would take bids for the sale of the buildings in the town, Tyre submitted what they considered to be the best offer.

Tyre purchased over 250 buildings, both commercial and residential. Soon he sent crews to Manning to tear apart all but a few of the structures in the town. The men filled one hundred railway cars with used lumber that Tyre sold for reuse as salvage building material. Thus Manning provided over two million board feet of used lumber that went into structures in Lufkin, Dallas, and Houston.

Today when visitors arrive in Manning, they find only one intact original building. This is the two-story white-painted wooden home of former sawmill superintendent W. M. Gibbs. On the far side of the mill pond behind the house, the concrete foundations of the sawmill lie silent, almost hidden beneath the verdant East Texas vegetation.

"Zero" Ervin, Texas Freedman

Born a slave in Louisiana about 1855, Felix "Zero" Ervin would be forgotten today by everyone except his descendants were it not for historian John N. Cravens. In 1972 Cravens wrote a biographical sketch of the former bondsman for the East Texas Historical Journal, and his life story deserves repeating.

"Zero" Ervin came to Texas after being freed from slavery by federal troops following the Battle of Mansfield, Louisiana, in 1864. He and his family migrated to Douglass in Nacogdoches County, Texas, shortly thereafter, and he lived in Nacogdoches, Houston, and Angelina counties for the remainder of his life.

Entering agriculture as a young man, Ervin worked for white people for the remainder of his days. We know that in 1887 he had begun working as a tenant farmer for the John L. Bailey family at Wells,

Texas, and by this time he had married his wife, Elnora, another former slave from Louisiana.

In appearance "Zero" Ervin was about average height and weight. Historian Cravens remembered, "He was very black and had a loose piece of skin on his neck." Throughout much of his adult life, Ervin kept a small mustache on his upper lip, shaving himself once a week with a straight razor.

Complaining as an adult that he had never wanted for clothing when "as a slave as a child, Ervin wore a felt hat summer and winter. During cold weather he wore a coat and wool trousers, while in the hot summertime he generally chose thin, often tattered attire, especially if he were working."

Though he worked for white people all his life, Ervin by no means exhibited "subservient" characteristics. Among the black population of East Texas, he was known as "a mean Negro." He would fight anyone who chanced to cross him.

Once Ervin somehow got into an argument with a young white housewife for whom he had been chopping firewood. The high tempered woman picked up a large stick and threatened Ervin, who responded only by raising up his hands to protect himself from an expected blow. "You might kill me, but you won't eat me!" Ervin exclaimed to the surprised woman. While the words of the housewife swearing that she would never employ him again were ringing in his ears, Ervin calmly walked away.

A few days later Ervin returned to the woman's woodpile, cutting up a huge pile of stovewood. Then, according to historian Cravens, "He sat on the chopping block until the housewife called him in for his breakfast. Thus the feud was ended."

Remaining healthy for most of his life, Ervin began to suffer from rheumatism in his elderly years. During his later years he lived with his daughters. It was while in the home of daughter Clara that he passed away from pneumonia on August 16, 1936.

A locally owned truck served as a hearse to carry Ervin's wooden coffin to the New Center Prospect Baptist Church near Pollok in Angelina County for his funeral service. Afterward his mortal remains found rest beside those of his wife in the nearby cemetery. Today their graves may be found there, marked with a single thin piece of plain marble, pushed by hand into the ground, surrounded by persimmon sprouts and tall grass.

Instructions for a Whipping

"You will go with Ralph home & see that you or Mr. Walton give him a good whipping." This is how the letter begins.

On October 5, 1859, Samuel Fountain Mosely from Linden, Texas, wrote to a man identified as "Brother Fox" back home in Jefferson, Texas, to give careful instructions for the punishment of Ralph, a runaway slave.

One-third of the Texas population counted in the census of 1860 was composed of black slaves. Texas had a total of 604,215 people in that year, and fully 182,921 of them were African Americans who lived in bondage. Ralph was one of these bondsmen, and he had tried to escape.

Writing about Ralph, Mosely said, "He tells me he ran away to keep Mr. Walton from whipping him." So afraid of overseer Walton's whip was Ralph that when other slaves came to deliver him to Walton for a beating, "he drew his knife on them & got away."

At some point in time, Ralph was captured, and Mosely employed Fox to deliver him back home to Marion County. As part of his job, Fox was to punish the slave.

"I wish you to go and see .that this matter is attended as it should be," Mosely asked Fox. "Do with him as if he were your own."

Fearing that Fox might injure Ralph severely in the disciplining, Mosely warned, "I do not want him scar[r]ed & cut up nor whipt unmercifully as part of his punishment."

At the same time that Samuel F. Mosely wrote his letter of instructions to Brother Fox, he wrote a letter to his wife as well. The wives of slaveholders participated in the institution of slavery just as their husbands did. Whenever the white menfolk were away, .the women had to take charge.

He advised her concerning the "treatment" of Ralph and the other slaves that the Mosely family owned. "I am again troubled about the . . . conduct of the Negroes," Mosely said. "In the absence of your father, I have written to Brother Fox to see that Ralph is properly attended to." Mosely admonished his wife, "You must look to the treatment of the Negroes and if necessary send for Bro. Fox."

The slave-owner seemingly was dissatisfied with the services of his overseer. He told his wife, "I have no confidence in Mr. Walton's treatment of the Negroes . . . and I know that he is cruel to them." He then added, "I want you to see that he does not cruelly whip any of them."

Although he showed a measure of concern toward his chattels, Samuel Mosely clearly wanted Ralph to be punished. He didn't hesitate to include chains as part of the punishment: "Tell Mr. Walton to put the handcuffs on him every night until he becomes humbled."

Life in antebellum Jefferson was not just mint juleps and magnolia blossoms.

The Ghost of New Birmingham

Visitors to New Birmingham today do not see very much except for the stabilized ruins of the Tassie Belle iron furnace, a few historical markers, and pine trees, but it wasn't always that way.

New Birmingham just south of Rusk, Texas, once was the industrial boomtown of East Texas. During its heyday a century ago the town had not only two operating iron furnaces, but also fifteen brick commercial buildings, a total of approximately four hundred residences and buildings, electric lights, street railways, and fifteen thousand people.

The story of how this metropolis rose and fell goes back to one Alexander B. Blevins, an Alabama sewing machine salesman who learned of the availability of vast amounts of iron ore in the area. Since 1884 the viability of smelting iron ore with charcoal in East Texas had been demonstrated at the Old Alcalde iron furnace at the Rusk state penitentiary, where the convicts provided the labor force, so Blevins knew of the feasibility.

The Alabaman conceived the idea that he could promote the establishment of a commercial iron foundry as the center for a new industrial town. He convinced his brother-in-law, an attorney from Calvert, Texas, to furnish him with money to secure options on the purchase of several thousand acres of land, and then he traveled to the East to enlist capitalists to back his project. Having chartered the Cherokee Land and Iron Company in March 1888, he successfully sold stock in the amount of one million dollars. The new company then purchased twenty thousand acres of selected iron, mineral, and timber land.

Having laid out the city, Blevins's company began selling lots in the town of New Birmingham on October 12, 1888, and they sold briskly. An amazing number of people came to the town with the expectation that they would get in on the "ground floor" of a major boom.

The first of two iron furnaces, the Tassie Belle, went into blast in 1889 with a capacity of fifty tons daily. It took its name from salesman Blevins's wife, and she cut the ribbon into the plant the day it opened. Two years later the nearby Star and Crescent furnace went into operation, and New Birmingham began producing iron on a comparatively large scale. Other businesses included an ice plant, pipe factory, brick works, bank, planning mill, newspaper, and steam laundry.

New Birmingham met its demise from economic causes. The first was that it was behind the times with its furnaces smelting iron ore with charcoal in a day when more efficient coal-based coke was supplanting it all across the country. The backers of the furnaces lacked the capital necessary to weather economic hard times, and they began with the Panic of 1893. The recently passed Alien Land Law made it difficult for the company to secure willing investors overseas for a venture in Texas.

Then, if the other woes were not enough to contend with, the charcoal beds and power plant at the Tassie Belle furnace burned in an explosion, and the company could not pay to have them rebuilt. People began leaving New Birmingham in what resembled a stampede.

By the beginning of the twentieth century, almost all evidence of New Birmingham had disappeared. Even the abandoned buildings were demolished for their materials to be used for construction in Rusk. The last intact building, the four-story Southern Hotel, burned in 1926, and its shell was demolished in 1932 to make way for a highway.

Nowadays the site of New Birmingham is crossed by the business route, U.S. Highway 69, on the extreme south side of Rusk. When you are in the Cherokee County area, stop by, take a look at the historical markers and marvel that you are standing in a place that a century ago was an East Texas boomtown.

Old-time Texas Kissers

While reading along, looking for other material in *The Texas Republican* newspaper published in Marshall, Texas, in the 1850s, I found something I didn't expect to find: a how-to article on kissing, 1854-sty1e.

You'd think that articles of advice on matters as intimate as this wouldn't have appeared at least until the twentieth century, but such is far from the reality of the past. So, what did *The Texas Republican* for June 17, 1854, have to say?

"Hardly any two females kiss alike," penned the male author of the article. "There is as much variety in the manner of doing it as in the faces and manners of the [female] sex."

The author, perhaps the Marshall editor himself, complained that the 1854 kissing situation was "a sad aggravation." Giving examples of the annoyance, the writer complained that some "delicate little creatures" merely gave their gentlemen friends slight touches of the lips. To this he peevishly grumbled, "We seem about to have a good time, and actually get nothing."

Contrasted were other ladies, who the Marshall writer described as going "into us like a hungry man into a beefsteak, and seem to chew up our countenances." He observed that this over-enthusiasm for osculation resulted only in driving away "delicate lovers."

Yet other sweethearts, according to the Marshall writer, were "like hens when burying themselves in the dry dirt." He then explained, "The kiss is won by great exertions, and is not worth as much as the trouble it costs." Women and men both could easily have uttered this complaint. After describing these extremes in smooching, the gentleman writer turned to advise his female readers: "We are in favor of a certain shyness when a kiss is proposed, but it should not be continued too long."

"Let there be soul in it," he continued.

The writer earnestly recommended that ladies "should be careful not to 'slobber' a kiss, but give it as a humming bird runs his bill into a honeysuckle, deep, but delicately."

"There is much virtue in a kiss when well delivered," added the writer. Such kisses he contended could provide memories to last a lifetime. "We have had the memory of one we received in our youth last us forty years," the Texan declared, adding, "we believe it will be the last thing we shall think of when we die."

Afraid of Water in Time of War

The Runaway Scrape was the incident in 1836 when Anglo-American settlers fled eastward in front of the armies of Mexican general Santa Anna during the Texas Revolution. The settlers realized that if they could manage to cross the Sabine River from Texas into Louisiana, they would be able to seek the protection of the U.S. Army stationed there.

"We knew that it meant our salvation to get across the Sabine," remembered J. H. Greenwood, who as a boy was one of the war refugees. He reported that everyone grasped the necessity to flee, "so . . . they needed no urging to hurry."

One of the impediments the escapees encountered was the Neches River. Under normal conditions a languid stream, the Neches in April 1836 had flooded over its banks, its turbid water covering the valley for about two miles across. With the Mexican army thought to be advancing on their rear, the refugees found themselves trapped against the flood-swollen Neches. Complicating the situation for the runaways was fear of attack from Cherokee Indians encamped in substantial numbers nearby.

"We had no boat and to cross without one was impossible," Greenwood related. "Refugees had continued to pour in until there were now more than three hundred families waiting to find their way across the stream." In desperation the settlers used what tools they had to begin fashioning rude ferries to carry their vehicles and most valuable possessions across the river.

Once the boats were built, the throng of settlers discovered that the little vessels could be used only on the deepest part of the river, that between the two banks. Otherwise they would drag bottom. The settlers had to wade a mile through the shallows to the deep water, then ferry across that comparatively short distance, and then wade another mile or so to dry land on the east side. "To see fifty or more families wading through the mud and water . . . was a sight long to be remembered by all present," Greenwood stated. The process eventually took three days.

One of the most prominent individuals involved in crossing the Neches was a woman remembered as Mrs. Moss. Her husband being an invalid, she served as the effective head of her household. While the settlers bivouacked on the west bank of the river and the boats were prepared, her pet dog, Rule, became a favorite in camp.

When the time came for Mrs. Moss to cross the Neches, Rule was not to be found. Finally as the boat was pushing off, Mrs. Moss spied her pet, jumped back to shore, and grabbed up Rule into her arms. She sprang back to the boat but missed, falling into the muddy water. Rule escaped from her grip, but Mrs. Moss managed to catch the dog by the tail "to which she clung for dear life."

Finally dog and mistress were drawn into the makeshift ferry, Mrs. Moss blowing water from her nose and wiping her face with her wet apron. Taking a firm grip on Rule's collar, she turned to the side of the boat and "proceeded to plunge him overboard, du[n]king him time and again." Greenwood remembered her words many years later: "I'll larn you, sir, to be afraid of water in time of war."

Freighting Cotton to Houston

N. B. Barbee of Crockett, Texas, knew the Lone Star State well, for he came to Texas as a four year old in 1841. He even remembered the day five years later that it formally entered the United States in January 1846. "I was at school at . . . San Augustine," he stated. "I well remember the ceremonies of pulling down the Lone Star flag that floated over the main building and the replacing it with the Stars and Stripes."

Barbee grew up mostly in the Crockett area of Houston County, where the majority of the people engaged in raising cotton for their livelihood. Much of the fiber, once it was ginned and baled, was taken downstream by steamboats on the Trinity River to the Gulf of Mexico for shipment elsewhere, but the stream was not always a dependable avenue of transportation because of frequent low water.

"At such times," Barbee noted, "planters who had piled their cotton on the banks of the river got tired of waiting for a rain and proceeded to wagon it to Houston." He explained that most of the cotton planters from the Crockett area southward preferred to sell their cotton in Houston, even though there were competing steamboat ports and cotton markets available at Jefferson and Shreveport.

Hauling cotton overland 125 miles or more to Houston was no small job. "Six yoke of oxen could haul a wagon with ten bales of cotton on it," Barbee reported, but the return of the teamsters home frequently was slow, much slower than might be expected. "Teamsters were often many weeks on a trip to Houston, for they usually did not return till they got a home load." In other words, if the freighters could not get a full load to carry back home, they would load up with goods destined for some other location perhaps as distant as Waco or San Antonio, neither of which had railway connections until many years later. They would haul goods anywhere they could until they chanced to load up with things destined back to Crockett. Then they would go home.

One of Barbee's family teamsters was a slave remembered as Uncle Jeff. According to Barbee, the bondsman might be away for as long as several months, "but he always got back with the money." The slave rode a pony as he drove the oxen, while another teamster rode along in the wagon. "He hauled eight or ten bales of cotton at a load and got $10 a bale for it," Barbee stated.

Freighting cotton remained commonplace among Houston County farmers until well after the Civil War and the arrival of the railway in Crockett in 1872. This event, however, drastically altered things.

Barbee reminisced, "The coming of the railroad . . . changed the transportation system, doing away with wagons as freighters and putting the teamsters out of business."

The days of long-distance cotton hauling for Houston County residents had come to an end.

My Dear Ichabod

While reading through old Texas newspapers, from time to time you find what literary people call "burlesque romances." They are purported love letters that our Victorian forbearers wrote and published in the papers for their own and others' entertainment.

One of my favorite such epistles appears under the title, "Caroline's Love Letter," on the front page of the Clarksville, Texas, *Northern Standard*. The Red River Valley paper published the letter on Wednesday, July 8, 1846.

Caroline's missal of love begins with the exclamation, "How I want to see your big grey eyes!" The love-stricken writer next launches into a series of entreaties to entreaties to her sweetheart: "Oh, sweet Ichabod, now do come out and let us get married if you love me. God bless you, if you are not sufficiently blest in being so sweet." And next comes a series of Caroline's pet names for her beloved. "Oh you marry-gold, you hollyhock, you tulip, you cabbage. Oh you sweet owl, do come and comfort your dying, sorrow smitten Caroline," she writes.

The letter continues to express the lover's loss at Ichabod's absence the preceding two months, which for her seems to have been more like an eternity. "Your dear presence would to me be worth more than the cooling spring to the parched traveler in the desert," she yearns. To the lonely girl, dear Ichabod means more than "a lump of sugar to a spoiled child."

To resolve the loss she feels, again, Caroline beseeches, "My Dear Ichabod," her beloved: "Oh, sweet Ichabod, now do come out and let us get married if you love me. God bless you, if you are not sufficiently blest in being so sweet." "Why then, will you not come, yes, fly as swift as the lightning to kiss the tear from the dimpled cheeks of your mad love?"

For Caroline, Ichabod represents the ideal of manly perfection. "Oh, you trim, tall fellow, full of manna of sweet love, how I do want to see you," she writes. Certain attributes especially attract her. "I do love your big red lips," she states unequivocally.

More pet names follow in closing the epistle of tenderness: "Oh, yes, bless thee, my dumplin,' my all, my rooster, my gentleman."

Perhaps best expressing her emotions, Caroline summarizes her feelings with the desire, "I want to see you and feel your heart bump."

And . . . remember . . . all this was in 1846.

Showtime in Henderson

In 1870 Colonel Lewis Ginger led an Iowa-based circus to Texas, but he nearly lost his shirt in the process. Only the good will of the people of Henderson saved the remnants of his show.

A one-third owner of the circus, Ginger and his partners brought it into Texas across the Red River at the Preston Crossing near present-day Denison. Stopping at most of the county seats along the way, he toured in a generally southwesterly direction through Austin and San Antonio. Business was good.

When the show reached the Gulf coast at Corpus Christi, however, disaster struck. Most of the circus horses came down with an unfamiliar disease—and this was in the days when horses pulled all the circus wagons. With only poor replacement horses, the troupe could not make the scheduled stops that had been advertised ahead. Then rains began that made the travel even slower.

"Finally at a small town where we were advertised to show, we came in two days late," Ginger related. He and his two partners decided that they had lost enough money in Texas, so they would simply divide up among themselves what few resources they had left.

"I was awarded the band wagon, a very elaborate affair . . . the six horses that drew the wagon and had escaped the disease, two baggage wagons and the mules to pull them," the businessman remembered. He made arrangements with the minstrel singers and musicians from the circus to accompany him in an attempt to get back home to the Midwest.

Before long the ragtag remnant of the circus made it to the town of Henderson in East Texas. The band wagon and its heavy draft horses created quite a stir in the little town on pulling up to the hotel. According to Colonel Ginger, "Soon a crowd gathered and made inquiries as to who we were," to which he answered that they were "the debris of a circus company."

The locals asked if the minstrels would be willing to perform since they were in town anyway, and the county sheriff piped up, "We have the large courthouse hall which we will be glad to let you have." With such an offer and nothing else to do that evening, Ginger, his minstrels and his two teamsters hastily put together a temporary stage and prepared to entertain whoever might come.

"We gave them a really first class entertainment," Ginger related, and the show could not have been a greater success. A member of the audience unexpectedly stood up and cried out to the rest of the crowd: "I think our citizens will be glad to help you out of your difficulties if you will pass among us and accept contributions from us."

Ginger himself had been playing tambourine with the minstrels, so he stepped down from the stage and circulated among the audience. "Those bighearted Texans filled to the top my tambourine with silver and gold," he remembered. The money was enough to carry Ginger and his crew on to Shreveport, where they were able to sell their baggage wagons and mules.

A steamboat from Cincinnati had just unloaded a cargo of goods to go up the Red River, and its captain had little to carry back. He let Ginger board his band wagon, draft horses and a hostler to care for them—all for the cost of just cabin passage for Ginger and his wife. The boat carried the party back to Cincinnati, "where I sold the wagon and harness to a circus company just ready for starting out and the horses brought me a good price."

"So that," he stated, "terminated my circus venture in Texas."

Texan Saw Stars Fall

"It looked like millions of stars were shooting down to the ground," Julia Palmer Roberts remembered from the great meteor shower of 1834.

Julia Roberts had been born in Shelby County in deep East Texas in 1820, and she was a teenager the night that the stars fell. "We were eating supper, when suddenly I decided to go out on the front porch and get a drink of water," she related many years later. "When I opened the door, I was startled by streaks of fire flying in every direction." The night sky looked almost as if it were on fire from the scores of falling stars.

Near the house was a pig sty, and from the teenager's perspective, "it seemed like most of the stars were falling right on top of our hogs." Julia screamed for her father, and the whole family rushed onto the porch to witness the celestial spectacle.

"For a moment Father gazed at the scene of falling fire," she remembered. "I could see his face as the flashes lit up everything, and it had a look I shall never forget." The father advised his family that undoubtedly the world was coming to its end. "We had better have a little prayer meeting," he said. They knelt together in the light of the falling stars, and, as Julia recalled, "Father asked the Lord to help us."

When I first read Julia Roberts's story of the night of the falling stars a quarter century ago, I thought to myself that a phenomenon as prominent as the one that she observed must have been seen by others. I went to my friend, Don Garland, who for years operated the planetarium at the Fort Worth Museum of Science and History, to ask him about it.

"It was definitely a meteor shower that she saw," Don responded. "It was not a single event, but one that lasted for some duration. . . . We know from the date what happened. We can trace it back to a particular meteor shower called the Leonids."

Not being an avid star gazer, to me this sounded remarkable. Don continued, "This is a meteor shower that takes place every thirty-three years." He went on to explain that at this interval the earth intercepts the debris from the ancient comet, Temple. As Don put it, "the meteors fall like rain." He explained, "Every thirty-three years this happens in the middle of November, around the 17th, at least the 16th, 17th, and 18th. We can pin her remembrance to a three-day span in 1834."

I asked Don whether Mrs. Roberts's story was exaggerated, and he said it probably was not. "The most recent occurrence of the Leonids was in 1966," he stated. "It was reported that there were at least two thousand meteors a minute. . . . No doubt what they were seeing in 1834 was of equal intensity. It definitely would have made an impression on them. It would on me if I saw that many of them."

"What about the next time?" I asked.

"There will be three sleepless nights for amateur astronomers in 1999 when they come again," Don answered. "I can guarantee that we will be out with our lawn chairs."

No doubt he was watching.

VI.

PRAIRIES AND LAKES

Courtship at the Cow Lot Gate

In 1904 Newton C. Duncan of Wheelock, Texas, told a tale of old-time Texas at the annual meeting of the Old Settlers' Association of Bell County. When I read it, I thought that it deserved retelling.

Duncan prefaced his remarks with an explanation that the Republic of Texas in 1837 granted to all men who had fought in the Texan Revolution land in payment for their services. As soon as the men received their grants, if they were single, most of them started looking for wives as helpmates in settling on the land. Before long just about all the eligible females were either married or engaged.

Duncan remembered one man named Sam who received his discharge from the army a little later than most of the other soldiers, and by the time that he returned home virtually all of the ladies and girls in the vicinity were committed to other suitors except for an older widow, Mrs. Sikes. Later Sam found a girl named Lizzie who was much more to his liking than the widow, but Lizzie played hard to catch.

On one occasion Sam met Lizzie at the gate to her father's cow lot, where the girl was milking the family's cows. Lizzie shut the gate, keeping Sam on the outside. Leaning over the gate, he told her that he had come on serious business and wanted to talk with her, proceeding to enumerate all the inducements that he could think of for her to marry him, including his land grant. He finally admitted to Lizzie that there was no one left in the neighborhood but herself and the widow Sikes.

"Well, why didn't you take the widow, Sam?" queried Lizzie.

In response Sam explained that he had found three objections to wedding the widow. "Wa'al, I found on close examination she had lost an eye," he said, continuing, "then she's red-headed, roman-nosed and worst of all, she smokes a gourd-neck pipe that will hold half a plug of tobacco, and I have always had a horror of being burnt."

Lizzie said that she thought Sam's judgment was probably sound, suggesting that she had cast her eye on him before. "I've been thinking something about getting married an' I reckon I had just as well begin talking about it now as any time," she said.

Lizzie then stated that she would consider marrying Sam, but only on three conditions: "You've got to make me three promises; first, that you won't drink whiskey; second, that you won't gamble; and last, that you won't ride a pitching horse."

Sam said that he could easily agree to the first two conditions, but the third one presented some problems. "I've already promised Major Golden," he replied, "to catch some buffalo calves for him next spring, and mighty nigh all his horses pitch."

Lizzie apparently concluded that two promises out of three was pretty good so she went to the house, talked with her parents about the match and agreed to marry Sam a few days later.

Thus the courtship at the cow lot gate came to fruition before the judge when Sam and Lizzie became man and wife.

An Irishwoman's Memories

"We left Dublin, Ireland, on the good ship *Quebec* in 1853," remembered Mrs. A. D. Gentry when interviewed at Fort Stockton, Texas, almost one hundred years ago. As a child with her family, she sailed first to Liverpool and then on to New Orleans, the trip taking over three months.

Having lost her mother to yellow fever at New Orleans, in April 1857 the little girl was sent to live with family members in Belton, Texas. She sailed from New Orleans to Galveston on the *Swamp Fox* and then spent about three weeks in Houston awaiting her relatives, who carried her to her new home in Belton in May.

"We made the journey from Houston to Belton in a buggy," she remembered. "It was in Belton that I saw my first biscuits and cornbread," which she considered "very unpalatable." Soon she learned otherwise, and in time she came to relish both.

After the outbreak of the Civil War, the young Irishwoman made do with only the barest of necessities. "Our coffee was made of parched wheat and our cake we sweetened with honey, for there was no sugar to be had, and at times we made tea from live oak leaves," she said.

The women of Belton militantly appropriated many of the items that they needed for housekeeping. When they required cotton fiber for spinning, they stopped the government wagons hauling it and confiscated what they needed from protesting drivers. "When we had obtained all that we needed, we told them to drive on," she reported. On one occasion during the war, six hundred pairs of cotton cards were delivered to a mercantile firm in Belton. "The women just went down and demanded that the cards be given to them, as they had to have them and had no money to pay for them," she said, adding, "This was done though with grumbling consent."

After the close of the war, the young woman married J. J. Greenwood and moved to the frontier near Lampasas, Texas. There she found herself again forced to rely on her own resources. "We cooked on an open fire in huge iron [Dutch] ovens and pots," she noted. From the heat of the cookfires, she remembered, "a woman needed no rouge . . . to render her complexion a carmen shade."

Everything that the family used required tremendous amounts of labor to produce. Candles, for example, were made at home from the tallow rendered from the fat of butchered cattle. "To make the tallow hard," she explained, "we used our own manufactured beeswax, making a mixture which answered every purpose."

On the frontier, Mrs. Gentry made an entire suit of clothes for her husband from scratch, spinning and weaving the fabric from a mixture of cotton and wool and sewing it entirely by hand. Reflecting on her efforts, she reminisced, "It was not at all a bad looking suit for that day, and I marvel now when I look back and I wonder how I did it."

Texas Fur Trade

When one thinks about the fur trade, ordinarily one thinks of the Rocky Mountains and the intrepid mountain men at their rendezvous. Certainly the Brazos River of Texas doesn't come to mind, but the fur trade once flourished there.

Seventy years ago historian Eugene C. Barker discovered in the Nacogdoches Archives at the Texas State Library an 1832 letter that sheds important light on the day-to-day life of Texas fur traders. In the letter Indian trader Francis Smith wrote from Fort Tenoxtitlan, on the Brazos River in present-day Burleson County, to A. G. and R. Mills in Brazoria, Texas. More than anything else, the letter presents a want list of goods that Smith needed for the coming summer trade.

On March 11, 1832, Smith reported trading with a Frenchman for eight tanned buffalo robes, with American hunters for cattle hides, and with Cherokee, Shawnee, Delaware, and Kickapoo Indians for beaver pelts. "My cart is now loaded with beef hides, deer skins, buffalo hides & robes, some leopard [cougar] & beaver," Smith reported. "My oxen are tied to the wheels and are to start for Brazoria tomorrow morning."

Among the goods that Smith expected to need for the Indian trade were such varied items as silk handkerchiefs, fishing lines, spurs, small check pattern calico cloth, straight awls, tin cups and pans, pocket knives, axes, and tomahawks. Not all the goods Smith had received had been satisfactory. "I have found that the common strouding is not good for those beaver hunters," he said. "They will not wear but tolerable broadcloth."

Trader Smith also wanted a good wagon to transport his furs and peltries. "Please . . . send to Cincinnati for a first rate large ox wagon for the road with . . . tires not less than 2 inches wide." He continued, "I cannot do without it. I am willing to pay the price, but I want one that will please me. I have the money laid by to pay for it."

Smith's Indian customers were often particular about their wants, and he attempted to meet their desires. He wrote, for example, "French or Mackinaw blankets is all the sort that will sell here." Another place he complained, "the keg tobacco I cannot give to the Indians. I have sold wine several times [but] it has been returned as often."

The shoes he received were especially unsatisfactory. "Those prunella shoes would never sell here. They have two faults: no heels & square toes. Please never send me any square toes. I send you [back] one dozen of them and keep the half dozen not to be without shoes. I think they may last me 17 years if I take good care of them."

In closing his letter, Smith expressed the frustration he felt in being so isolated at his post on the Brazos. "I do not know how to get my money to you. I cannot shut up and go down, for I am the only one that has anything to sell of consequence."

The Gainesville Cyclone of 1854

Eight-year-old Tommy and nine-year-old Louise Howeth, brother and sister, lie side-by-side in the Fairview Cemetery at Gainesville in the Red River Valley. Their graves are in what today is Division D in the burial ground, in front and south of the chapel. The thing that sets them apart from the other people there is that they started the cemetery.

The story of Tommy and Louise goes back to the evening of Sunday, May 28, 1854. They were in the home of their parents, Mr. and Mrs. William Howeth, together with an aunt and uncle and their two children. The Howeths lived on the fringe of settlement, their home being one of the handful that had been built west of Gainesville.

In May 1854 Gainesville was barely a town. When W. B. Parker visited the community a few weeks later, he described it as being a "collection of five or six log cabins, dignified with the name of a town."

On the evening of May 28, 1854, the sky darkened and the winds began to rise as a typical late springtime convectional storm brewed toward the west. W. W. Howeth, then a boy, later recalled, "A tornado was forming, and in a few minutes . . . reached from the earth to the cloud above, with all its blackness, whirling and roaring."

Having nowhere else to seek shelter, the two families all huddled in William Howeth's cabin. Little did they imagine the force that the cyclone was about to exert. The entire house was blown down upon its inmates, killing all of the children but one. The two wives were so severely injured that their lives were threatened.

Other frontier families in the Gainesville area suffered as well. Mrs. William C. Twitty and her stepsister, a Mrs. Olivo, had spent the Sunday visiting in the home of Mrs. Twitty's father, Daniel Montague. Late that afternoon, as the two ladies headed for their respective homes, the clouds darkened and the thunder began to rumble.

The Standard in Clarksville, farther down the Red River Valley, reported that the homes of both the Twitty and the Montague families were "uprooted . . . even the bed clothes torn to shreds by the force of the wind." The storm struck after Mrs. Olivo had returned home, and she saved her children from its fury only by "placing them in a small cellar under the floor," although she herself was seriously hurt.

In the same neighborhood, James Rutledge suffered damage to crops and home. "The roof of his house was blown clear away and has not yet been found," reported the paper.

Some of the damage was incredibly gruesome. When he passed through Gainesville shortly after the storm, W. B. Parker noted "a horse was blown into a tree, where it happened to catch by its fore-leg and shoulder; these were torn from the body and were still hanging there, the balance of the carcass lying in a field a full quarter of a mile off."

Summarizing the devastation at Gainesville, *The Standard* described the cyclone as having been "a gale unparalleled save by the hurricanes of the tropics" . . . and that it was.

The Greek Engineer at the Compress

John Bohopolo was his name—the Greek engineer at the cotton compress in Gatesville, Texas—and R. L. "Uncle Bob" Saunders knew him well. A century ago Saunders worked as a grease monkey for Bohopolo at the Southwestern Compress Company in Gatesville.

Large-scale cotton cultivation came to Coryell County after the Civil War. Farmers from other southern states migrated there, settling in the river valleys where the bottomland proved especially fertile. The rich soil in the bottoms averaged producing a bale of cotton to the acre. Since most of the farmers had big families, they had ready supplies of labor to pick the harvest in late autumn and winter.

With increased cotton production, it was necessary for the Coryell County raisers to ship it to market as inexpensively as possible. In 1882 the Cotton Belt Railway came to Gatesville, and soon its trains began relieving the situation by hauling hundreds of cotton bales to market. A difficulty that the shippers encountered, however, was that the bales not only weighed five hundred pounds apiece but they also were bulky. Gatesville had no compress.

A cotton compress is an industrial machine which exerts high pressures to mash cotton bales together tightly for shipment. A compressed bale measures only about half the size of an uncompressed bale. The economy of transportation for compressed bales is obvious.

Not long after the arrival of the railroad, the Southwestern Compress Company of Tyler, Texas, built a compress adjacent to the Cotton Belt tracks in Gatesville. The complex included a long, raised wooden loading platform with the compress machinery near its center. An office stood at one end, while the boiler producing the steam power to operate the heavy machinery was at the other.

The Tyler firm sent Earl Fain to supervise the new compress, while it employed John Bohopolo, the Greek engineer, to run the steam equipment. Integral to the successful operation of the compress were six black workers, all of them highly skilled, who the company also sent to Gatesville from Tyler. They were the "press men" and the "truckers," responsible for keeping a steady flow of bales moving to and from the compress machinery on hand-drawn four-wheel carts called "trucks." Martin Payne and George Johnson were the two press men, "and they knew their business," Saunders related. Overseeing the work of the truckers, Payne and Johnson kept a steady stream of trucks in motion when the press was running. When Payne called for more cotton, the truckers according to Saunders "would sure go in a long lope" pulling their cotton-laden carts.

With Fain supervising the overall operation of the compress and the black laborers moving the bales of cotton where needed, engineer Bohopolo ran the steam equipment. "He was the man that pulled the levers that controlled the pressure rams," Saunders said.

Bohopolo came to Gatesville from Goose Creek in Harris County, and like most Greeks, he loved the sea. "He used to tell me," Saunders related, "that when he wasn't working as a compress engineer, he owned a boat and fished and smuggled quite a bit . . . in the Gulf of Mexico."

Having lived on the sea, the Greek had learned many of the English language oaths of mariners, and he rarely hesitated to use them to get results. "Believe me," Saunders said, "everybody stepped lively when old man John Bohopolo screamed a few of them deepsea curses."

The Greek engineer was as striking in appearance as he was in behavior, every day wearing a black wool broadcloth suit and a white shirt open at the collar. "When he pulled the pressure levers, he had on gloves," Saunders remembered. "He was dark complexioned, and with his handle bar mustache and all them glad rags that he wore," Saunders declared, "John Bohopolo was a sight to behold."

He is still remembered in Gatesville.

Letters from the Republic

"Kind moments afford me an opportunity of writing," is how Milly Talitha Rawlins began a letter back home to Illinois from the Republic of Texas in March 1845. A transcript of her letter is preserved with others from her family in the Center for American History at the University of Texas.

Milly Talitha Rawlins was a teenaged daughter in a group of relatives and friends that her father, Roderick Rawlins, organized in 1844 to emigrate from Illinois to the Republic of Texas. The party consisted of Rawlins, two sons and five daughters and their families, as well as several friends.

They located on Ten Mile Creek on the west side of the Trinity, being the first settlers in the vicinity. "Our nearest neighbor is seven miles [away], except those that came along with us," Milly Talitha Rawlins wrote. Her father, Roderick, noted similarly that "There was no settlement . . . until we came."

Another family member, Polly Rawlins, in a contemporary letter, described the new home in Texas: "I am very well pleased with the place that father has settled on," noting, "I think it pleasantly situated. . . . We are in a tolerably good house and have enough to eat." About this home,

Milly Talitha Rawlins commented, "We are at this time in a comfortable house. [It] has two rooms to it.

The setting impressed Milly Talitha Rawlins more than her new home: "We are close to a beautiful spring which affords us plenty of water. We are in the prairie on a tolerably high place, all around as green as a wheat field. The prairies are beautiful, high and rolling."

The location in Dallas County, according to Milly Talitha Rawlins, afforded abundant wild game. "Buffalo can be seen by thousands in the prairies about 20 miles from this place, and deer and turkey to any amount. Wild bees are found plenty." The presence of predatory animals didn't seem to concern the teenager. "Panthers, bears [and] wildcats are tolerably plenty and wolves to any amount," she wrote.

The abundance of fish in the Trinity River, half a dozen miles away, was a great bonus for the new settlers. Milly Talitha Rawlins reported, "I have told you about all I can except about the fish. There are thousands of them in the river. We have lived on them and buffalo for some time, and the men are going this evening to catch more."

Roderick Rawlins wrote home predominately about the agricultural prospects of the land, expecting more friends and family members to join him on Ten Mile Creek. "The prairie land," he noted, "appears to be of superior quality to any I ever saw in any other country." He added, "The soil is as deep or deeper than that of Illinois and of a darker color."

Giving suggestions that other immigrants might follow, Rawlins had some very specific advice: "Prepare as well as possible. Have good horses, wagons and harness and try to have double the money that you think would answer," adding that en route, "Don't stay too long in St. Louis."

Answering criticisms that he had heard in Illinois about the character of the settlers moving to Texas, Rawlins reported to his family members back home, "I have not seen in any country . . . a more friendly, intelligent people than I find here."

Daughter Milly Talitha Rawlins lonesomely wished for more teenaged companions. "I see but little fun here for girls," she lamented. Living in a frontier society in which men greatly outnumbered women, she observed, "Girls here are very scarce, but [as for] young men or old ones, . . . there are more than you can shake a stick at."

George Jackson's Multi-colored Britches

Pioneers came to Texas not just from adjoining areas but from all parts of the world. George Jackson and his family, for instance, immigrated to Texas from England in 1848.

According to the emigration agent who had encouraged the Jackson family to come to the new world, Texas was a land of "one continuous spring and summer . . . with no chilling winds or driving snow." After they arrived and built a 12- by 14-foot log cabin about fifteen miles from Dallas, as chance would have it, they suffered through the winter of 1848–1849, which was one of the most severe experienced in the region.

After several months on the Texas frontier, the Jackson family grew more and more shabby looking. George Jackson, then a boy, later remembered, "the clothing we brought from the old country began to get very seedy and full of patches and minus many buttons." Coming from developed and industrialized Britain, neither George's mother nor his sisters knew how to spin and weave cloth at home, a skill that greatly aided American homemakers on the Texas frontier.

In order for them to look presentable at a summer 1849 camp meeting, George's father purchased his three sons new white canvas trousers from a store at Farmer's Branch. While the parents left for a day or two at the camp meeting, promising to take the boys there next, the boys discussed their new garments.

"After they had gone, we boys held a council and discussed our new white pants," Jackson remembered. "We considered them very common and thought we were entitled to something better." Bill, one of George's older brothers, came up with a solution to their perceived problem. Having observed American neighbors dying cloth brown with green walnuts, he suggested that they do the same with their white trousers.

While Bill went out on horseback with a big sack to collect the nuts, the two younger brothers built a fire and began heating water in a large iron washpot. By the time the water had heated, Bill returned with about a bushel of green walnuts, dumping them into the vessel. "After stirring them for a while, we took off our pants and put them in the kettle of dye and began a steady stirring among the walnuts," Jackson said. Each boy agitated a long stick with his trousers attached. Dressed only in their shirts, the three boys walked around and around the steaming cauldron, working the mixture in order to insure even color distribution.

All went as planned until the boys suddenly were confronted by a well dressed lady visitor. Embarrassed by being caught without their trousers, "We hastily fled to the corn patch nearby and hid there until she departed."

Returning to the washpot full of walnuts, steaming water and three pairs of pants tied to sticks, the boys were more than dismayed. "We found them changed into garments of variegated shades, here and there with a streak of yellow, and a streak of brown where the walnuts had rested while we were hiding in the corn."

Having no other trousers to wear, for the next months the three Jackson boys were seen around Dallas County in multi-hued pants. George Jackson concluded, "There were black spots as big as marbles in various places, and our newly dyed pants would well have matched Joseph's coat of many colors." This was the last time that the Jackson boys tried dying their clothes.

Of Oxen, Bacon Rinds, and Whiskey

Driving ox teams in freighting across pioneer Texas was hard work requiring skill and experience, both of which qualities teamster George Jackson exhibited. He freighted between Jefferson and McKinney in the years preceding the Civil War. Jackson had come to Texas as a boy immigrant from England in 1848, growing up in the Farmers Branch area north of Dallas. As soon as he became old enough as a teenager to take care of himself, he became a teamster.

Freighting was a good business in Texas during the 1850s. There were very few railroads, all of them in the southeastern part of the state, leaving the rest of the state dependent on either steamboats or wagons for heavy hauling. Jackson remembered that teamsters generally averaged earning between $3.00 and $3.50 per hundredweight to transport goods to the Dallas area from either the steamboat landing at Jefferson or from Houston.

In hauling a load of merchandise from Jefferson to McKinney, Jackson once had the unfortunate luck for one of his oxen to go lame. He was a member of a party of freighters traveling together. "There was quite a train of us," Jackson recalled, "and every wagon had 4000 to 5000 pounds of freight."

The teamsters had an unwritten rule of aiding any of their number who chanced to have misfortune on the road. Jackson explained, "The teamsters were rather rough, but they were true to one another and would never desert a companion in trouble."

The entire party, consisting of several freighters with their wagons and about thirty yoke of oxen, determined to stop for two or three days while Jackson's animal recovered from its lameness. Then one member of the party, remembered as being a very ingenious Yankee, declared, "Hold, hold, let me suggest. . . . Boys, let us shoe that ox."

"We have no leather or anything else to shoe him with," replied another member of the party. The Yankee then proposed, "We have a lot of bacon sides and we can shoe him with bacon rind." No one had ever heard of making animal shoes from the skin cut from sides of bacon, but the men were game to give it a try. "Some bacon was hauled out of the wagon and a piece larger than a dinner plate was cut off for each shoe," Jackson related, "and we went to work like experts making shoes for that ox."

The teamsters made four bacon rind shoes, attaching them to the feet of the ox, and they proved to be a good fit. Then one of the freighters took out his whip to make the animal get up and try its new shoes.

The resourceful Yankee interrupted, "Boys, let's give him a dram of whiskey." Already the men had tapped the best barrel of whiskey in the train of wagons, so they drew from it a quart bottle full. While one of the men held the animal's nostrils and another held its horns, a third poured the liquor down its throat. "The old ox licked out his tongue, smacked his lips and got up," Jackson reported. "For a while he was as frisky as a young colt with his new bacon rind slippers and morning dram."

Shod and intoxicated, the animal was ready to proceed. Jackson concluded, "He felt so elated that he tried to pull the whole load, and our long train of freight wagons moved slowly toward McKinney, which we reached in due time."

French Utopia in Dallas

On the north-facing slope of a limestone hill that overlooks the Trinity Valley on the near west side of Dallas lies a wholly unexpected site. Here, between present-day Hampton Road and Westmoreland Avenue, French immigrants in the 1850s founded the utopian colony of La Reunion.

Most of La Reunion has been literally blasted away by the Portland cement companies that have quarried limestone from the hillside to be used in concrete production, but a few traces remain. Up on the top of the hill near a historical marker for the colony in Stevens Park is Old Orchard Drive, its name deriving from a fruit orchard there in the days of the colony. Then, down in the valley, diagonally across from L. G. Pinkston High School, are the historic tombstones in La Reunion colony cemetery.

What brought the Frenchmen to Texas?

The immigrants were all adherents of a socialist philosophy propounded by François Marie Charles Fourier, a prominent French thinker of the nineteenth century. Interpreting what he considered to be the natural order of society, Fourier asserted that utopia could be created by placing people into cooperative communities in which everyone worked for the good of the whole. The settlements proposed were not purely communistic, for the members were permitted to own private property, but they were strictly organized to work for the benefit of the community.

La Reunion was one of several Fourieristic communal settlements that were established in the New World during the 1850s. Explaining for others Fourier's philosophical basis on which La Reunion had been founded, its Texas leader, Victor Considerant, compared the French immigrants to the Puritan founders of Massachusetts in the 1620s. "Our position, with the difference of two hundred years, is that of your Pilgrim Fathers, who settled New England," he wrote. "Europe is declining, is rotten. America has a space without limits, a future without shackles. . . . The best elements of the Old World ask only to leave it; let America afford them a little aid!"

Come the French immigrants did, settling on the limestone hillside and living more-or-less communally. The first party of approximately two hundred arrived in April 1854, and they were followed by additional parties over the next two years.

The colonists were not the best suited to rural Texas, for many of them were intellectuals more familiar with urban life than with herding cattle, plowing fields, and building fences. Many of the newcomers left La Reunion almost as soon as they arrived, but for a while others came to take their places.

La Reunion failed as a communal settlement because of lack of satisfactory leadership, mismanagement of its financial affairs, the failure of nearby Americans to participate in or to encourage the colony, and the inability of the settlers to agree among themselves on what they should do. Gradually La Reunion melted away in the late 1850s and early 1860s. Some of its settlers returned to Europe, others moved to French-speaking New Orleans and a handful remained in the Dallas area, where their descendants remain today.

The name of the ill-fated socialistic colony perpetuated from 1980 to 2008 in the downtown Dallas Reunion Arena, where hundreds of thousands of spectators gathered to cheer their favorite teams in sporting events and to attend public entertainments. Ironically the crowds in the arena that keep the name of La Reunion alive never imagined that it came from Fourier's French communistic colony on the banks of the Trinity.

The Toad of Toads

In an open, plush-lined miniature coffin in a display case in the Eastland County Courthouse in Eastland, Texas, lies a Texas "horned toad." This in itself may seem a little bizarre, but the tale of how the lizard found its way there is even more remarkable.

The story of Old Rip, the embalmed lizard that lies in the little coffin in Eastland, goes back to 1897. In that year Eastland County built a new courthouse to replace one that had burned. Will Wood, a boy growing up in the town, gave to his father a horned toad that he had been playing with, and the father dropped it into the cornerstone of the building on the day it was to be dedicated.

The folklore at the time was that a horned toad (or any reptile, for that matter) would go into a form of suspended animation akin to hibernation if it were enclosed from light and air. Wood was curious to learn whether the lizard could survive inside the cornerstone.

The pink granite stone, also containing a Bible, newspapers, and other memorabilia, was duly sealed during the ceremony in autumn 1897, and everyone forgot about the lizard—everyone except for the members of the Wood family. Thirty-one years passed.

When Eastland County began construction of a new courthouse in 1928, it was necessary to remove the old building from the site. Over a thousand people came to see the proceedings when the old 1897 cornerstone was ceremonially opened on February 28, 1928.

Edwin T. Cox, who was present at the time of the ceremony, reported later that several feet of brick had to be cleared away before the top of the cornerstone was exposed. According to Cox, "First to be removed from direct contact with the walls of the cavity in the cornerstone was a piece of galvanized iron which snugly fitted the top of the cavity."

With the iron cover detached, the officials then removed the newspapers and other articles. "I then saw one of the party reach down and bring to sight a horned frog which, seemingly, was dormant but after a few moments showed signs of life," Cox wrote.

Another witness to the event later stated regarding Old Rip, "The judge held him up, dangled him in the air, holding him by one leg for everybody to see. And then, the other leg twitched, and somebody shouted, 'My God, he's alive!'"

Alive he was, and within days the Texas lizard became breakfast-table news for the whole United States due to the promotional efforts of Eastland newspaper editor Boyce House. Thousands of people flocked to Eastland to view the amazing animal that purportedly survived thirty-one years sealed up in a cornerstone. Certainly critics asserted, with strong scientific evidence, that no horned toad could live so long without air, food, light or water, but no one in Eastland would accept their arguments.

For the next several months Will Wood, who rightfully claimed ownership of the lizard, toured with him around the United States. Old Rip drew forty thousand viewers to see him at the St. Louis Zoo, where the president of the St. Louis Zoological Society offered one thousand dollars to anyone who could disprove his authenticity. In the nation's capital, Will Wood and Old Rip went to the White House to see President Calvin Coolidge. "Silent Cal" stroked the lizard's back with his horned-rimmed glasses, and according to the press, "the President and Old Rip gazed steadily at each other for a full minute."

Old Rip's career as a touring novelty came to an untimely end on January 20, 1929, just less than a year after he had been recovered from the cornerstone. His head was found protruding from the soil and leaves at the bottom of the glass bowl in which he had been kept. "Apparently the recent sunshine had lured him from the protection of the earth and sand," the local newspaper reported, "and he was chilled to death." The official cause of death was listed as "pneumonia."

Was the "Toad of Toads" a hoax or genuine? When you visit Eastland, examine for yourself the pink granite cornerstone from the 1897 courthouse where he reputedly spent his thirty-one years. It stands beside the sidewalk on the north side of the current seat of justice in town. Today the cavity holds nothing but rainwater during wet weather, but it purportedly once held Old Rip.

A quarter century ago, when I asked Eastland County Judge Scott Bailey what he thought about the remarkable lizard, he told me, "I have to give a lot of credence to it. I've talked to a lot of old timers who saw it."

The next time you have a chance, go to Eastland yourself and have a look.

Sophia Porter, a Pioneer of Texas since 1835

On a hill overlooking Lake Texoma, which now covers the ghost town of Preston on the Red River, one finds one of the most appealing cemeteries in Texas. Amid the oaks and evergreens of the Preston graveyard about ten miles north of Pottsboro, lies the grave of beautiful Sophia Porter, the Texas Confederate spy.

Born in 1813 at Fort Wayne, Indiana, Sophia came to Texas in 1835 as the teenaged bride of a teacher named Jessie A. Aughinbaugh. They arrived just in time for him to desert her during the Runaway Scrape in the Texas revolution, but Sophia didn't remain single long. Soon she caught the eye of a trader named Holland Coffee, and they wed at Washington-on-the-Brazos in 1837. Sam Houston was one of the guests at the ceremony.

The newlyweds moved to a stockade trading post that Coffee had built at Preston, one of a series of such posts that he had established in the Red River Valley. In time Coffee built for Sophia a home called Glen Eden, a two-story structure with galleries across the front, which, according to a local historian, "represented the ultimate in luxurious living for that era." Unfortunately Coffee was killed in a duel at Preston in 1846, leaving Sophia a widow.

After Coffee's death, Sophia remarried Major George Butts, although this marriage lasted only a few years due to the untimely death of Butts. In 1865 Sophia married a fourth and final time, on this occasion to Judge James Porter of Waco. The Porters lived in Sophia's big house on the Red River at Preston for the remainder of their lives.

Although Sophia was reputed to have been one of the most glamorous women in early day Texas, she is best remembered today not for her beauty but for her services as an espionage agent for Confederate forces in the Red River Valley during the Civil War. She repeatedly garnered military secrets from conversations with officers and men from Union commands that occasionally patrolled the area, passing the intelligence on to Texan authorities.

Once Sophia saved Confederate commander James Bourland, who was responsible for the border area along the Red River, from apprehension by a larger body of federal troops. The blue-coated men unexpectedly appeared at the door of Glen Eden seeking information on the whereabouts of Bourland. Sophia knew that Bourland and his men had just passed through Preston on their way to Fort Washita and were in danger from the federals.

Sophia hosted the Union men at Glen Eden overnight, opening her wine cellar to them and entertaining them until late into the evening. While the evening's merrymaking was at its height, the adopted Texan stole into the darkness to warn Bourland. Since all the horses were at range in the pastures, she feared that if she tried to catch one of the mounts there she might be observed. Consequently she saddled and bridled a mule in her own barnyard, swam it across the Red River and rode to catch up with the rebels to warn them of their imminent danger. That very night she quietly returned to Preston without being discovered, undoubtedly saving Bourland from attack.

Preston remained the home for Sophia and her fourth husband until his death in 1886. As the matriarch of Glen Eden, she survived him another eleven years, herself passing away in Preston at the age of eighty-three in 1897.

Sophia's spire-like marble tombstone in the cemetery on the hill above the former town still reads for all who care to see, "Sophia . . . Porter, a Pioneer of Texas since 1835."

Refugees Travel to Texas

Mrs. I. M. Williams came to Texas from her Arkansas home in 1864, but her coming was not a pleasure trip. Her husband was fighting for the Confederate Army in the Civil War, and she and her sister traveled with thirteen black slave children to escape fighting and privation in Arkansas.

"We had three yoke of oxen, 2 wagons and 13 Negro children to take to Texas," Mrs. Williams related. Her older sister, Matt, drove one of the ox-drawn wagons, while Mehala, a black matron, drove the other. Mrs. Williams herself rode ahead on horseback to lead the way and to search out food for the group.

Travel was difficult. "We were heading toward Little Rock through rain and snow . . . when my baby took sick," she related. They made camp near a military camp at Paraclifta, Arkansas, and on the second night the baby died. "I rode horseback to the soldier camp and had them make his coffin and bury him," she said.

When Mrs. Williams returned to sister and slaves, she discovered that a passing group of soldiers had killed Mehala, who had faithfully driven the second wagon. The slave had laughed when her mistress's pet dog, Fido, had snapped at the heels of the troopers' horses. "I had to go back to Paraclifta for soldiers to come to camp and wrap Mehala in a blanket and bury her by the side of the road," she remembered.

As Mrs. Williams and her party continued toward Texas, "We were nearly starving," she stated. They had eaten no meat for days and days, having only cornbread and sorghum molasses. Finally she spotted some wild hogs, and with Fido she cornered two of them that she killed with an axe. Dragging the carcasses to camp with an ox and a log chain, Mrs. Williams and her sister butchered them. "They looked as pretty as any hogs I have ever seen," she declared, adding, "We began broiling livers to feed the hungry children and before we went to bed that night we had the hogs' heads and feet cooking."

One more day's ride brought the Williams party to the Red River at Colbert's Ferry near present-day Denison. It was too late in the afternoon for the ferry to carry them across the river, but the ferryman advised Mrs. Williams where the water was shallow enough for the oxen to cross. "I rode one steer and drove one of the wagons while Sister Matt rode a steer and drove the other wagon and we got over the water all right," she remembered.

The group continued on to the area of Clarksville, Texas, where they stayed for the next months until the Confederate surrender in April 1865.

Reflecting on her experiences in travel as a Civil War refugee to Texas, Mrs. Williams years later concluded, "That is how Sister Matt and I carried our 13 Negro children to Texas."

A Texas Cowboy on a Minneapolis Mule

S. H. Woods of Sherman, Texas, later a prominent attorney in Alice, Texas, began his employment career as a cowboy working for the Suggs Brothers in the Chickasaw Nation of the Indian Territory.

In July 1881 Woods became a horse wrangler on a trail drive that moved about three thousand head of steer yearlings from the Suggs Brothers' Oklahoma ranch to another ranch the brothers owned in Wyoming.

After three months on the trail, the herd reached its Wyoming destination. There the crew received a second herd of cattle. These animals were ready for market, so the cowboys drove them northward to Glendive, Wyoming, where they were loaded onto cars of the Northern Pacific Railway.

From Glendive the crew rode on the cattle train with the Suggs Brothers' animals to Chicago, but on the way they had a lengthy stop at St. Paul, Minnesota. "While the cattle were resting, we all took the interurban street car for Minneapolis, about 5 miles from St. Paul, to see the Barnum & Bailey circus," Woods recalled.

The Texas drovers attracted as much attention from the audience as the circus performers when they entered the big tent show "still wearing trail garb."

Just as they found their seats, a clown in the ring began offering five dollars to anyone who could ride his trick mule. "Twelve Texas cowboys fresh from the range thought that was easy money," according to Woods, "and all wanted to win the $5.00, so, we selected one of our party to earn the money." The circus performer accepted the cowboy challenge. "The clown let out his mule and we let out our Texas cowboy," Woods said.

In preparation for the competition, the clown tied a blindfold over the eyes of the mule and permitted the cowboy to mount up. "When the word was given," Woods remembered, "one of our boys pulled off the blindfold, halter and all, and left the two of them in the ring ready for business."

The big audience witnessed the subsequent head-to-head contest between the cowboy and the mule, the Texan clinging for dear life and the animal doing all it could to dislodge its unwanted rider. Woods related, "The mule made two or three jumps and reared like a mountain lion, and our rider yelled like a Comanche Indian." The animal pitched and bucked, even rolling onto its side, "but our rider stuck to him like a postage stamp." The ride lasted far longer than either mule or cowboy had expected. "The audience went wild and uncontrollable and the police had to interfere and pull our rider off the mule."

Woods concluded, "The $5.00 was given the rider, and after the performance we returned to St. Paul, reloaded our cattle, and continued our journey to Chicago, where we delivered them and left for Texas."

Woods didn't say whether the five dollars made it to Texas or not.

Horse Thieves or Spies? Nobody Knows

Less than a mile from where I live in the country, about halfway between Waco and Fort Worth, grows a giant live oak tree beneath which stands a grey granite marker. I've known the big tree all my life, and it marks the spot where, as my grandfather related to me, "The Spaniards killed Philip Nolan."

"Who was this Philip Nolan?" I used to ask when I was a little boy, but all I could learn from my grandfather was that Nolan was an American who had come into Spanish Texas a long time ago to capture wild horses. The nearby Nolan River, my elder explained, had been named for him. Twenty years passed before I discovered that the story of Philip Nolan had been told by one of his men, Ellis P. Bean, in a narrative published in 1855 as part of Henderson Yoakum's two-volume *History of Texas*. The story goes something like this:

Philip Nolan was an American "mustanger" who had come to Texas as early as the 1790s to capture wild horses in order to sell them back in the United States. In 1800, for example, he returned from the Trinity River in Texas with 1,300 captured mustangs which he sold at Natchez,

Mississippi. Later that year in Washington, D.C., Vice President Thomas Jefferson interviewed Nolan as an expert who could tell him about the Spanish territory west of the Mississippi.

In late 1800 Nolan with a party of about twenty men returned to Spanish Texas. Some people in Natchez said that he was traveling as an espionage agent to explore and map Spanish territory for the U.S. government. Others asserted that he was planning to trade with the Indians while trying to locate supposed Spanish gold and silver mines. Yet others reported that Nolan was simply going to catch more mustangs for the lucrative horse trade in the Mississippi Valley. No one really knew.

Whatever the reason for the trip, Nolan and his men reached the area of the Brazos River in Texas sometime in late 1800. "We found elk and deer plenty, some buffalo, and wild horses by thousands," Ellis Bean later wrote. In the vicinity of what today is called the Nolan River in Hill County, they built a small wooden stockade fort in January 1801. This structure with nearby horse corrals became their base camp.

Pursuing the mustangs, Nolan and his men spent some of their time with a roving band of Comanche Indians. The Americans, however, were encamped at their stockade when they were surprised by about 120 Spanish soldiers from Nacogdoches sometime before dawn on March 21, 1801.

After apprehending all of the men who had been posted outside the stockade to guard the horses, the Spaniards left only about a dozen of Nolan's men inside the fort. "We were all alarmed by the tramping of their horses," Bean wrote, "and, as day broke, without speaking a word, they commenced their fire."

In the ensuing battle, leader Nolan was slain by a gunshot to the head, while two of his men fell wounded. The troops fired both with muskets and with a small swivel gun loaded with grapeshot.

After Nolan's death, Ellis Bean took charge. He told his comrades they could save themselves only if they took the swivel gun or if they retreated. Only two or three men favored assaulting the field piece, all the others preferring retreat. Filling their powderhorns to capacity with gunpowder, they placed the remainder of their ammunition in the hands of Caesar, one of two black slaves who had accompanied the American expedition.

"So we set out through a prairie, and shortly crossed a small creek," Bean said. "While we were defending ourselves, Caesar stopped at the creek and surrendered himself with the ammunition to the enemy."

The remainder of the party sought shelter in a deep ravine, where they successfully defended themselves for a while longer, eventually running short of gunpowder. About three o'clock in the afternoon, the Spaniards sent out two men under a white flag of truce. One of them, an American trader from Nacogdoches named William Barr, related that the Spanish commander had requested their surrender, adding that since Nolan had been killed, the Americans would be released to return to the United States.

One by one the mustangers surrendered, and they returned with the soldiers to Nacogdoches. There the Americans waited a month for orders expected from Mexico City to set them free, but, as Bean remembered, "instead of our liberty, we were seized and put in irons and sent off under a strong guard to San Antonio," from which place they were marched to prison in the interior of Mexico.

Only one of the Nolan party ever made his way back to the United States alive, and this was the Ellis P. Bean who left the account of the expedition. Had Bean not returned, today we probably would know very little about the Nolan expedition of 1800–1801 and its fate beneath the live oak trees that still grow along the river that bears Nolan's name.

Ben Bickerstaff Dead or Alive

The town square at Alvarado in Johnson County is a quiet place, but it wasn't always that way.

When you go there, you see at the center of the square a white gazebo erected by the high school senior class of 1979, while around its manicured lawn and behind parking spaces stand commercial buildings. Many of the old buildings have been replaced by redi-built metal structures with brick veneers, but a few of the old ones hide just behind clean-looking false fronts.

Some of these walls heard the gunshots on April 6, 1869, when Alvarado wasn't so peaceful. This was the day when Texas desperado Ben F. Bickerstaff overstayed his welcome in Alvarado.

A native of an area just east of Sulphur Springs in Hopkins County, Ben Bickerstaff as a young man served in the Confederate Army before returning home following the Civil War. Like many veterans, he never was able to fit back into the humdrum routine of civilian life. He gradually changed from a local bully into a thief and finally into a full-blown desperado with a thousand dollar dead-or-alive reward on his head.

Bickerstaff reputedly murdered his first man in Louisiana, where he shot a former slave. Fleeing federal officers there, he returned for a while to the Sulphur Springs area, gathering about him a band of thugs. He soon became involved in violence directed toward the Union Army of occupation in Texas.

When things grew too hot at Sulphur Springs, Bickerstaff moved a hundred miles southwest to Alvarado. By this time he had assumed the name Thomason as an alias and had become partner of another hoodlum confusingly named Thompson, who originated from Alvarado.

A. J. Barnes and David and John Myers, all of Alvarado, described for the press the problems Bickerstaff created. They complained that Bickerstaff and his chum visited the town "in the evening and during the night to institute a carnival of robbery and other crimes" and that as time passed, "the criminals became bolder, and their outrageous acts grew to be more unbearable."

Finally the local residents took all the abuse that they were willing to stand. The press reported, "the good citizens of the village prepared themselves with shooting apparatus for the purpose of ridding their community of these, the greatest pests they had ever known."

As daylight on April 6, 1869, changed to dusk, the merchants stationed themselves near the doorways of their stores. According to their custom, the two outlaws rode up on their horses. Observing the men retreating inside their stores, Bickerstaff called out derisively, "Rats to your holes!" followed by profanity.

The two desperadoes proceeded to a hitching rail and dismounted. "So soon as they had alighted," the press reported, "a shower of death-dealing leaden balls was directed at them." Thompson, hated by the storekeepers even more since he came from Alvarado, fell in the first volley, killed instantly.

Bickerstaff remained game, notwithstanding three gunshot wounds—one of them in the right eye. "He fired two well aimed shots," according to the press, "one ball passing through the clothes of one of his adversaries, and one shot striking a gun in the hands of another." He continued shooting at random until he exhausted his ammunition.

A crowd then gathered around Bickerstaff as he lay dying, propped up on his elbows in the dirt. He conversed with the townspeople, cursing his partner for dying so easily. Just before he himself expired, the outlaw explained to all who could hear, "You have killed as brave a man as there is in the South."

The story might end here, but it didn't quite. The citizens of Alvarado did receive the one thousand dollar reward that they had hoped to earn for Ben Bickerstaff dead or alive.

Wandering John Taylor

Strange stories grew up about strange people, and early Texas had more than its share of unusual individuals. One of them was itinerant lawyer "Wandering John" Taylor.

In order to preserve the memory of Wandering John, one of his legal associates, W. D. Weed, penned his remembrances of the nonconformist attorney for publication in the quarterly of the Texas State Historical Association in January 1900.

Weed first met Wandering John Taylor at the spring session of the district court at Centerville, Leon County, in 1852. He remembered, "A gentleman on horseback, with three led horses, tied head to tail, tandem fashion, packed with blankets, provisions and camp equipage, rode down to the creek nearby, and in the shade of some trees where grass was plenty, proceeded to dismount, unpack and stake his horses." This was Wandering John.

Taylor was a handsome man, six feet tall, erect, and well proportioned. Weed described him as having "an eagle eye, a kind and pleasant face and a graceful carriage."

As Taylor traveled from courthouse to courthouse, he seemingly needed no more home than the hospitality of shade, grass and water, for he had little to do with any ether members of the human race except to practice law wherever chance happened to place him. Usually this was in the areas of Cherokee, Andersen, Houston, Leon, Robertson, Madison, Limestone, and Freestone counties.

Without announcement Taylor would appear in towns when court was about ready to go into session, set up temporary lodging at a campsite and await business. "He would attend the session of the court, and if he had or secured any business, he would remain until it was disposed of," Wood said. If Wandering John failed to find any clients, "he would . . . decamp as suddenly as he came."

Wandering John's legal reputation was based on his oral presentations in the courtrooms, for voice, gesture, and inflection were highly prized by pioneer Texans. To them the greatest lawyer was the most eloquent one. During criminal proceedings, most interest focused on the "pleading," and many locals for entertainment came to the courts solely to hear the attorneys "plead."

Wood described Wandering John's courtroom orations as being like "the impetuous flow of a swollen mountain stream." Attorney Taylor accomplished the effect seemingly without effort. "He never hesitated for a word, and every word was suited to the purpose he had in view," Wood said. A contemporary declared that Taylor's words bent the emotions of jurors "as the ripening corn is swayed and bent by the summer breeze."

It was unusual for Wandering John Taylor to sleep anywhere except in his open-air camp, where he found his only company among his horses. On one occasion, however, he shared a hotel room with W. D. Wood during a trial proceeding. "John and myself were assigned to the same room, and the same bed, as was often the case in those early days." After the two men had retired, Wood retreated from the bed on account of attacks from bedbugs, choosing instead to sleep on a blanket pallet on the floor.

"John seemed undisturbed in his position in the bed, and slept soundly," Wood said.

The next morning Wandering John arose and began dressing for the coming day in court. From his vantage point on the floor, Wood looked up as "two very large bugs, so full that they fairly glistened, crept into John's "pants pocket, as much as to say, 'Strange as you are, we like you, and we intend to keep you company.'"

Summertime Jaunt up the Brazos

A saddle trip up the Brazos Valley could be most pleasant in the spring or fall, but that wasn't what Dr. G. C. McGregor and his friends chose. Instead he and his companions set out from the Wesley community, southeast of Brenham in Austin County, in mid-June 1871. They made their way up the west side of the valley by way of Waco to Meridian and then came down the east side of the valley back home.

In 1947 historian Roger Conger rummaged through some old things in a home that was going to be torn down on Columbus Avenue in Waco, and in the trash inside the barn he found a little leather-bound book in which McGregor kept a journal of his 1871 trip up the Brazos.

"Left Monday, June 19th for Waco," he penned in the diary, noting the route of travel and the places stayed. On the very first day the party met trouble in crossing Yegua Creek in western Washington County, "where we came near sticking in the bottom of the river with the water up to the saddle skirts." After struggling through the mud, the men stopped for the night on a cotton farm. There the "man spoke slow," he wrote, "but his wife made up for his loss of speech" and only charged them fifty cents apiece for food, lodging, and pasturage.

Their route up the west side of the Brazos brought the horsemen to Cameron, the seat of Milam County, but they were unimpressed with what they found. "The land is poor and sandy—not fit to farm,"

McGregor commented, adding that "Cameron is a poor dilapidated town on a sand hill . . . [and] has not a speck of paint and all the gardens are grown in rank weeks."

They proceeded on up the valley, stopping on a farm in western Falls County near the Jeno community. "Here we stayed all night and got treated as well as circumstances would permit." After a week and a half in the saddle, in late June, McGregor reported, "we have in sight of Waco," where they spent several days resting up from their travels. The members of the party were all impressed with the "beautiful suspension bridge" across the Brazos, which only the year before had opened.

Next the horsemen set out northwestward from Waco, passing onto the prairies and spending the night at Valley Mills in Bosque County. The physician noted "there is a good deal of stealing about here," but he added, "the thieves are summarily dealt with." The seat of justice for the county, however, did not strike the visitors very favorably: "Meridian is a poor place with some 6 stores and a poor looking courthouse and rotten jail."

The party next headed east to cross the Brazos at the town of Fort Graham before turning southeastward toward home. They passed through Hillsboro, in the Blackland Prairie, which the physician described as "a pretty little town in the midst of a vast prairie as far as the eye could see."

They proceeded on to the Mt. Calm community in extreme southern Hill County, where the full blast of summer hit them. McGregor penned in his little pocket notebook, "The country [is] . . . very scarce of water and the thermometer as high as 101 degrees. Everything literly parched up."

The horsemen secured a meal on the virtually treeless Blackland Prairie outside Mt. Calm, "but the place was so warm that we left in the boiling sun to seek a cooler place, which we found in the shade of a few hackberries, where we stayed till late in the evening."

The summer heat apparently got the best of the young men, for they decided to make for Groesebeck, located on the Houston and Texas Central Railway. There they made arrangements to transport their horses back home to Brenham while they rode along in the railroad passenger coaches. Though they felt hot, McGregor lamented, "I could nearly cry for our horses, shut up in a close boxcar [w]here there was but 12 inches crack and thermometer 101."

The party finally returned home in mid-July, glad to be off the road. The trip, however, may have resulted in Dr. McGregor's relocation to Waco, for he resided there most of his later life, practicing medicine and investing in real estate. Today he is remembered most prominently for the town of McGregor, west of Waco in McLennan County, which bears his name.

A Faithful Knight of Labor

Just on the east side of Interstate 35, at the small town of Bruceville between Temple and Waco, stands an unusual tombstone. I first stumbled across it years ago, but only recently did I do my "homework" to find out about it.

The marble slab in the Bruceville cemetery commemorates the life of Martin Irons, the words "fearless champion of industrial freedom" chiseled into its side.

Who was Martin Irons? I wondered. Ruth A. Allen's book, *The Great Southwest Strike,* published in 1942, answered my questions. A Scotsman by birth, Martin Irons, almost in spite of himself, became the leader of the 1886 strike of workers against financier Jay Gould's network of railroads.

During the decade of the 1880s, Gould gained control of the largest network of railways serving Texas, Indian Territory, and Missouri. The lines included, among others, the Missouri Pacific and the Texas & Pacific.

Due to oppressive railway company policies, railroad efforts to reduce wages and company refusal to recognize the Knights of Labor (the largest trade union of the day) as a legitimate bargaining partner, union men went on strike in March 1886. Vocal organizer Martin Irons became the most prominent spokesman for the strikers in their inevitably unsuccessful fight against Gould's industrial might.

With the failure of the strike later in 1886, many of the union men were refused their old jobs and had to move on to non-railway employment or other places to live. For Martin Irons life became a nightmare. Blacklisted by the railways, he never again was able to find employment at his trade as a machinist. Wherever he went, his identity was discovered and old defeated railway strikers from 1886 sought him out to vent their bitterness over the failure of the strike. A reporter from the *New York Herald*, finding Irons in St. Louis after the strike, wrote: "This little man is now a ghost . . . the ghost of the dead hopes of those 14,000 men who were under his leadership."

In 1897 Dr. G. B. Harris, a social democrat and one of the wealthiest men in McLennan County, Texas, befriended down-and-out Martin Irons, whom he found in utter deprivation. Near his home in Bruceville, Harris erected a small house for Irons, and there the wanderer spent his last years.

When Irons was not "home" in Bruceville from his travels promoting the organization of workingmen, he often could be found on the front porch of a local store. When a Bruceville resident who knew Irons was asked in the 1940s whether the old agitator discussed social questions, the local replied, "He never talked about anything else."

Irons lived in Bruceville until his death from pneumonia on November 17, 1900. An obituary published in the Jefferson City, Missouri, *Daily Tribune* declared, "I wish I had the ability to sing the praise of the old man broken down who crept away to the border town of Bruceville, Texas, to die alone and penniless.

"With him died forever many of the secrets of the Southwest Strike," the writer penned, "for he ever remembered his obligation. . . . He died as he lived, a Knight of Labor, faithful even unto death."

The Preacher and the Phrenologist

In 1883 Professor Orson Squire Fowler came to Waco, Texas, and stirred up a hornet's nest of controversy that resulted in his hasty departure the next day.

Fowler was the most prominent popularizer of the nineteenth century pseudoscience of phrenology. Adherents of phrenology asserted that an examination of the lumps and bumps on the head could reveal all of an individual's traits of character. The reason for this, they believed, was that the brain was composed of multiple "cerebral organs" and that the relative size of these components of the brain as shown by the lumps on the skull indicated all of a person's mental and moral abilities and tendencies.

In the course of Professor Fowler's lecture, he explained to the audience the marvels of human character that could be shown through phrenological examinations. He then invited volunteers to come to the front of the hall for complimentary readings, the results of which, would be shared with the crowd.

Among the people to present themselves was a tall, well-built man with an apparent military bearing. The phrenologist allowed his fingers to feel all parts of the man's cranium, pronouncing to the audience, "This man is a skeptic on the subject of religion."

Throughout the hall audience members amazed the great phrenologist with their reactions, for some of them hissed, while others, seemingly insulted and aggrieved, quietly left. Only after the close of the lecture did Fowler learn that his volunteer had been Dr. J. S. Shaw, pastor of the Fifth Street Methodist Church. So discredited in Waco was Fowler, that he stole away to another stop on his lecture tour, all the time claiming the validity of his reading.

Several months following Professor Fowler's lecture in Waco, the Reverend Shaw began preaching sermons along the line of what in the twentieth century might have been termed "modernism." Becoming more and more adverse to the generally held views in his congregation, the minister finally told the stewards that he did not believe in the biblical miracles. Unwilling to serve as the pastor of a church espousing doctrines in which he no longer believed, Shaw left the Methodist faith and organized a group of freethinkers under the name of the Religious and Benevolent Association of Waco. From its auditorium the former minister waged relentless warfare on the Bible and all organized religion.

B. H. Carroll, the pastor of the First Baptist Church in Waco, wrote an especially effective sermon critical of Shaw entitled, "The Agnostic," and he delivered it from pulpits in many of the surrounding towns. After Carroll spoke in Gatesville, fifty miles west of Waco, newspaper editor J. B. Cranfill published it in the Gatesville *Advance*, printing several hundred extra copies for distribution back in Waco. The controversy waxed hot and heavy for months.

In 1885 Fowler returned to Waco, and this time the locals flocked to his lectures. The phrenologist's scientific expertise had been so vindicated by the events of the past two years that there was "standing room only" during his presentations.

J. B. Cranfill, the editor from Gatesville, attended one of the lectures and volunteered for a public examination. "He said that if I would keep my feet washed in the way he suggested and sleep out in the open air, I would live to be 80 years old," he remembered.

Years went by and all the participants in the freethinking controversies of the 1880s either died or moved elsewhere, when in 1927 editor Cranfill wrote an article about Shaw and Fowler for the *Houston Chronicle* Sunday supplement. In writing the feature, he assumed that the former preacher had passed away, having heard nothing about him for years.

Shaw, however, was then still living, and a friend sent him a clipping of Cranfill's article. The old freethinker wrote back to Texas:

"In view of the fact that Dr. Cranfill and I were so long active opponents on the question of religion and on other issues," Shaw wrote, "I am much gratified that he, thinking I was dead, spoke of me in the article . . . so kindly."

"Knowing me as he did," he continued, "he evidently thinks that being dead I am in Hell, but please tell him that I am in California, which all Californians think is very near Heaven." The ex-preacher concluded, "I am now in my 85th year and as far as I can judge in perfect health."

Old Days on Little River

"I was born in Lincoln County, Missouri, October 5, 1835," begins the autobiographical narrative of Susan Turnham McCown, which she dictated to her son-in-law in 1913. The narrative says much about pioneer life in Texas, for McCown told about her days as a girl on the frontier after her family moved there in 1840. McCown's father, J. J. Turnham, settled on the Little River in Milam County a few miles west of present-day Cameron. "At that time there were no settlers west or north of that place," she noted.

Initially there were only five families living in that area on Little River, but in spring 1842 they joined in building a log school. They then made arrangements for a Mr. Lampkin, one of the better educated from among the settlers, to become the teacher. The first school year began in May and ran through the summer to September. "The old house was so open" and drafty, remembered McCown, "that the children could not stay in it in cold weather."

The school furnishings were rude at best. The bench-type seats were made from split logs, while the light by which to read came from the sun shining through the cracks between the logs, there being no windows. Textbooks were in short supply, most of them being "those from which our parents had obtained their little education." Reflecting on the surroundings for the simple school, McCown stated, "Nature furnished the only free book, and it was open with its unsoiled pages full of absorbing interest the year around."

At school and at home, the children had to be aware of dangers. "We could play in our yard and watch the buffalo and bear come down to the river to drink," Mrs. McCowan remembered.

In addition to the wild game, the settlers and their children had to be aware of Native Americans, some peaceable and others not. "We had no shutters at first . . . , and often a shadow would fall across the doorsill, and we would see an Indian curiously peeping into the room," she said.

On one occasion all the children of the McCown household, both white and black, for the family had slaves, were entertaining themselves in one of the log houses by picking seeds from the season's cotton. In the days before there was a cotton gin, this was the only way that the fiber could be cleaned preparatory to carding, spinning, and weaving. As the children visited and extracted the seeds, according to McCown, "an Indian hand was thrust through a wide crack in the wall and a handful of our cotton disappeared."

This abrupt surprise put an end to the evening's work, the children scrambling to their beds and the men reaching for their guns. The alarm was false, however, for no harm had been intended. McCown related that the Indian had been prowling around the outside of the house when he saw the children at work picking out the seeds. "As he had never before seen any cotton," she reported, "he just reached in to get some for closer inspection."

Bill, Bob, and the Bull

John W. Lockhart, a longtime resident of the Brazos bottoms, used to tell a wonderful story about two Texas cousins, Bill and Bob, and the former's encounter with a wild bull.

The 1850s meeting between man and beast took place at Port Sullivan, which today is a ghost town on the west bank of the Brazos in Milam County not far from Hearne and Calvert. Bill had gone there from his home at Chappell Hill, Texas, to visit his cousin Bob.

Bob owned a general mercantile store in Port Sullivan which stood near one of the several saloons in the town. "It happened that a considerable crowd had gathered in front of the bar-room," Lockhart related in telling the tale. "Bill, having indulged in too much whiskey, . . . swore that he could ride anything that wore hair."

This boast couldn't go without response from the crowd of Port Sullivan loungers, who knew that a particularly large bull was grazing among a herd of Texas cattle not far away. One member of the group wagered Bill a five-dollar bill if he could ride a bull. "Bill, not knowing there was such a thing as a bull anywhere around, thought there would be no impropriety in taking the bet," Lockhart said.

Giving the other loungers a wink, the man who had wagered with Bill called on half a dozen of his cronies to ride out and rope the bull and then bring it around to the front of the saloon. When the men reappeared with the bull, "Bill was the blankest man that ever visited Port Sullivan," Lockhart stated. "If the bull had dropped from heaven, he could not have been more surprised."

Realizing his predicament, all created by his own boasting, Bill swallowed his pride and tried to wrangle out of his wager, but the crowd wouldn't let him back away. Now Cousin Bob's efforts came into play.

Pretending not to have heard any of the preceding ballyhoo, Cousin Bob walked up to the crowd, declaring to Bill's chagrin that no one should try to prevent Bill from riding the bull. He even swore that he would whip any man that would try to keep his cousin off the bull. Bill was aghast, feeling that his cousin was helping to offer him up for sacrifice for the entertainment of the Port Sullivan rowdies.

While the snorting animal was being prepared for the ride, Cousin Bob did all he could to prevent Bill from backing out of the ride. A rope was placed loosely around the bull's body just behind its shoulders, and the cowboys began loosening their lariats from the beast. "Amid the protestations of Bill, and the assertion of Bob that no one should prevent his cousin riding, Bill was lifted bodily and placed astride of the animal," Lockhart remembered. His knees were placed under the rope to prevent his being pitched backward, while the animal's tail was placed in one of his hands to keep him from being bucked off forward.

Amid the cheers from the Port Sullivan loungers, Bill began his high ride. As soon as the bull found itself free from its lariat entanglements, it began bucking and bellowing, setting up "a regular fore-and-aft movement" of one end up and then the other. Bill looked as if he were on a seesaw.

The bucking continued for several minutes, Bill holding onto the rope and the bull's tail. After a while the beast headed into nearby woods, but returned toward the town, Bill still astride.

The animal headed toward the bluffs of the river on which Port Sullivan stood, but the locals mounted their horses to divert the beast away from the steep acclivity and down a well-worn track to the banks of the Brazos.

When the bull reached the edge of the water, it jumped out as far as it could go. Bill turned a somersault off its back, landed in the water and swam for shore. As Lockhart ended his story, "Bill was the lion of the day and, with his five dollars and a host of admirers, spent a fine evening."

Fruitcakes from Corsicana

What do you think that Gene Autry, Sugar Ray Robinson, and the Mandarin Hotel of Singapore have in common? They are all customers of the Collin Street Bakery in Corsicana, Texas. This is the home of the DeLuxe Fruitcake, produced by the same firm for the past ninety-two years.

Today the fruitcakes from Corsicana are shipped annually to almost two hundred countries around the world. Annually the bakery produces about three million pounds of fruitcakes. They may indeed be one of the most famous Texas exports. When Tine Holm in Kolbotn, Norway, for instance, decided to order a fruitcake for her grandmother, she wrote out her order and put it into the mail addressed to "Fruit Cake, Texas." It went to the Collin Street Bakery.

The story of the DeLuxe Fruitcake of Corsicana goes back to 1896. In that year a German immigrant baker named August Wiedmann came to Corsicana. There he teamed up with a local capitalist named Thomas McElwee, and they opened a modest bakery on Collin Street. There Wiedmann perfected the holiday season fruitcake that is still produced. It is notable for the large amounts of pecans used in its making.

The business grew gradually for a decade before moving into new quarters in a two-story building at Collin Street and West 6th Avenue in Corsicana. Gus Wiedmann operated the bakery on the lower floor, while McElwee ran a rooming house on the second story. Never missing an opportunity to make sales, the two men actively promoted their bakery goods among the transient guests. Many of the travelers later ordered Wiedmann's fruitcakes through the mail.

Perhaps the largest boost to mail-order sales came after John J. Ringling and his circus troupe spent several nights in the rooming house above the bakery while performing in Corsicana. They subsequently ordered several hundred of Wiedmann's fruitcakes to be sent to recipients in foreign places.

The name of the Collin Street Bakery and the high reputation for its fruitcakes grew and grew, as did sales. After the death of McElwee in 1946, ownership of the firm passed to other local Corsicana businessmen, who continued using Gus Wiedmann's original 1890s fruitcake recipe. The business grew too great for the limited quarters of the old bakery on Collin Street, so in 1965 the bakery moved to a new location at 1300 West 7th Avenue, where it remains today. Its sales counter is open all day weekdays and Saturdays, and coffee still is only a dime a cup.

As I whiffed the tantalizing odors of the cakes and pastries at the sales counter, I puzzled over how such a prominent baking firm had ended up in Corsicana, which is not really on the most frequented paths of travel. When I wandered upstairs into the business offices of the bakery, I found out.

Two pretty receptionists were sitting at desks in the front of the offices when I told them that I was looking for information on the history of the bakery. One of them giggled and asked the other, "Do you think I should tell him about the train?" While I wondered what she meant, the other receptionist replied, "I don't see why it would hurt anything."

Then the first young lady related, "Gus Wiedmann was an immigrant from Germany." This I knew, but then she added that Wiedmann was wandering about the country as an unemployed hobo and chanced into town in a railway car. "He was kicked off a freight train in Corsicana," she chuckled, "and that's how he, got here." Whether the story is true or not, Texas for well over a century certainly has benefitted from Gus Wiedmann's "DeLuxe Fruitcake" recipe.

On the Road with Teamsters

Freighting became a way of life for many Texas farmers in the 1860s and 1870s, because they often had to use their own wagons and horses or oxen to transport their crops to market. Thomas U. Taylor, later a University of Texas engineering professor, was born in Parker County, Texas, in 1858, and he left his remembrances of the system.

On the open prairies west of Fort Worth, Taylor's family became successful wheat farmers. The marketing procedure that they followed was to transport their grain to local water-powered mills to be ground into flour, after which time they hauled the flour by wagon to the neatest railway point for sale.

"After the crops were gathered in the fall," Taylor explained, "every farmer made a trip to the end of the [Houston & Texas Central] Railroad, which at that time was slowly crawling across the state from Houston towards Sherman." As the railway construction progressed northward, the terminus of the line, called the "depot," gradually shifted from Millican (between Navasota and College Station) to Bryan, Hearne, Grosebeck, Kosse, and Corsicana.

"These depots," Taylor wrote, "to put it mildly, were 'wild and wooly.'" Gamblers thronged their streets, wagering not only on card games but on "every imaginable game of chance." Since Taylor was just a boy at the time, however, the older men kept him close to camp at night, so he failed to witness any of the frequent shootings, as "these happened late at night after I had retired."

One of the most difficult points along the freighting route for the teamsters was the crossing of the Navasota River bottoms. Taylor related that all the teamsters referred to the location as the "Navasot," with the accent on "sot." He declared, "'Navasot' . . . was the muddiest and boggiest piece of road . . . It took us nearly one day to get three teams across the Navasot."

All along the route of wagon travel, the teamsters camped night after night on their treks. The locations for campgrounds depended on the availability of wood and water—wood for campfires and water for animals and men. The "wagoners," as the teamsters at the time called themselves, always looked ahead for these two necessaries of life. "A few sticks of wood were always carried for an emergency, especially on the long trips over the prairies," Taylor recalled. During dry times the limited number of springs or dependable water holes became oases that attracted teamsters by the dozens, but usually only four or five freighters would camp at the same place.

Although the drivers might be from different locales, they nearly always had their meals together at night. "They built a common fire, brought their mess boxes, each one cooked his own food, and then they passed it around," Taylor said. Indispensable in such camps was a big coffee pot, described as "always on the fire, always full of coffee."

Freighters amazed young Thomas U. Taylor with their ability to drink the hot brew boiling hot. "I never saw a wagoner yet who would not use the half-pint tin cup, pour his coffee out of the pot into the cup, and drink it without waiting for it to cool off."

Two Hunters, One Bird, and a Dead Man

Whenever two hunters vie for the same game, tempers are sure to flare. When one hunter is black and the other white and the year happens to be 1868, real trouble might brew. This is just what happened at Weatherford, Texas, 143 years ago.

No one knows what really happened on Saturday afternoon, June 13, 1868, other than the fact that Joe Williams killed a stranger who was walking into town. Williams was black and the traveler was white.

According to sworn testimony by Williams, he had been hunting and took a shot at a bird that the traveler also was attempting to hit. After Williams frightened it with his gunshot, the other man started an argument over the bird, the white traveler reportedly kicking the black hunter. Williams claimed that after this assault, he shot the traveler in his own self defense.

Other people in the neighborhood reported that they heard only one shot, supposedly the one that killed the traveler, and that they saw Williams taking belongings from the dead man's clothes when they approached. Whatever the case, Williams realized that he had become a hunted man, and he disappeared into hiding.

Jeff Eddelman, another African-American resident of Weatherford, decided that he would try to capture Williams for the small reward that had been offered for his apprehension. Knowing that Williams had a great love for music, he had several black women come into his back yard to sing, while he secreted himself inside the house with a loaded gun.

True to form, Joe Williams appeared from the brush, and Eddelman ordered him to stand where he was or be shot. The fugitive turned to run, and Eddelman fired a shot that struck him in the arm below the elbow. Though wounded, Williams fled east and south from town, eventually being apprehended by a posse of local citizens after a twenty-five-mile chase.

After receiving medical attention for his injured arm, Williams was lodged in the Parker County jail in Weatherford to await trial. Several weeks passed with the black man incarcerated while the prosecution prepared its case against him. The court appointed a young attorney named George Clark, later Texas attorney general and an unsuccessful candidate for governor in 1892, to defend the accused man. Despite Clark's able defense, the jury on November 14, 1868, convicted Williams of murder, the penalty being death by hanging.

Accordingly on December 18, 1868, Williams was driven to the site of a makeshift gallows about two miles outside town, sitting all the way on his own wooden coffin as the wagon bounced along. Once at the site, the sheriff permitted him to address the assembled crowd as he stood on his own casket in the back of the wagon.

After complaining of the treatment he had received from the local law enforcement officers, Williams addressed the black members of the crowd, admonishing them to be careful to avoid his fate of falling into the hands of the law. "Be keerful," he said in a distinctive brogue, "watch whar you am gwine."

The driver then popped his whip and the two-horse team jerked the wagon from beneath Williams, leaving him dangling from the end of the rope . . . and to this day no one knows what really happened six months before when the two hunters argued over the same bird.

Fort Worth and the Buffalo

Today Fort Worth isn't associated with buffalo, but just over a century ago the near extermination of the bison contributed substantially to the economic growth of Fort Worth—"the town where the West begins."

Systematic destruction of the buffalo for its hides entered Texas from Dodge City, Kansas, where it had begun in 1872. European tanners had developed new methods for converting raw buffalo skins into useable leather, "the plastic of the 19th century."

After the June 27, 1874, standoff battle of hide men and Plains Indians at Adobe Walls, the Kansas hunters shifted their base of operations from Dodge City to Fort Griffin, Texas, on the Clear Fork of the Brazos just over one hundred miles west of Fort Worth. Although the slaughter took place miles to the west, Fort Worth with its railway connections was the place that most profited from the trade, which lasted through 1879.

Readers of the *Fort Worth Daily Democrat* learned on November 8, 1876, for instance, that "Freighters are wanted to transport buffalo hides to Fort Worth. The amount is the largest ever known. Countless herds of buffalo cover the prairies. Ten thousand hides are now on the way to the railroad and thousands await transportation to Fort Worth."

The city at the forks of the Trinity became the shipping point for the tens of thousands of buffalo hides that were taken on the western Texas plains. There was only marginal opposition to the slaughter, and precious little of it appeared in Fort Worth. "People may object to the wholesale destruction of these animals," the Fort Worth editor wrote on August 18, 1876. He noted, however, that after the removal of the bison, cattle "will be a source of greater wealth to the state than all the buffalo that ever trod the plains."

Fort Worth residents saw yet another advantage from the decimation of the bison. For years the settlers of western Texas had suffered the ravages of Indian war parties, but the plains warriors and their families depended on the bison for their sustenance. With relief the editor wrote, "with the disappearance of the buffalo vanishes the independence of the Indians. . . . The buffalo hunters are doing more to a solution of the Indian enigma than all the would-be wise legislation of Congress."

While the hunt progressed west of Fort Worth, its merchants reaped the real profits. Since virtually all the hides passed through the city, most of the hunters' proceeds eventually reached the hands of Fort Worth businessmen. The *Daily Democrat* happily reported to its readers on August 19, 1876, that "the buffalo hunters beyond Fort Griffin . . . have commenced their fall business of slaughtering the buffalo . . . there will be one thousand hunters at work inside of four weeks, and . . . double the number of hides will be shipped this fall."

The editor then added significantly, "Fort Worth will receive all the hides, and the trade of the liberal hunters, who spend money recklessly, and buy what they want regardless of expense."

Commerce in buffalo hides contributed heavily to the development of the city Texans today call their Cowtown—so much so, in fact, that in 1876 it might well have been known as Hidetown.

Amateur Road Agents

Everyone has to start somewhere, and Mary's Creek west of Fort Worth is where a trio of robbers apparently began its career in crime.

While reading through pages of the *Fort Worth Daily Democrat* for Sam Bass outlaw stories, I came across this little-known incident that gives some insights into the activities of the petty criminals who co-existed with the "big boys" in days gone by. Then, as now, there were plenty of petty punks for every notorious criminal. These boys represented the thug category.

The Fort Concho to Fort Worth stage was running late on the night of Friday, December 21, 1877. Because of heavy storms and high water south and west of Fort Worth, the driver didn't reach Mary's Creek until about an hour after midnight. This crossing was still nine miles outside Cowtown. The night was especially dark on account of the continuing rains.

As the driver directed his team across the bottoms, a trio of unknown men emerged from the rain and gloom and called out for him to halt. Like any driver with good sense, he did. Since there was no cargo of any particular value on the stage, the highwaymen ordered the passengers out onto the soggy ground. Into the mud stepped George Mellersh of Dallas and C. F. Shields of Coleman County, the only two passengers.

At gunpoint the two men turned over to the road agents a total of forty-six dollars in cash. This surely must have been worth more in

1877 than it is today, but even so it wasn't much of a haul for an armed robbery. The gunmen, however, didn't seem to blame their victims, for the next day the press reported, "the robbers gave each of the gentlemen one dollar to get breakfast with when they arrived in town."

After the highwaymen disappeared back into the darkness, the stage made its way the remaining few miles into Fort Worth. Soon news spread that there had been a robbery, and the *Daily Democrat* sent a reporter to interview the two victims.

The men reported that they had turned over to the road agents only token cash, as each of them had hidden in their clothes considerably more. Shields had successfully concealed two hundred dollars, while Mellersh had an additional "$700 on his person" as well as "a fine gold watch and other valuable property." As it turned out, neither of the victims really needed the dollar received back from the robbers.

About daylight in Fort Worth three "suspicious looking parties" were seen at the El Paso Hotel, but as no one could identify the robbers who had appeared in the gloom of the rainy night, the three men "were not disturbed."

Reporting on the incident, the newsman concluded that since the robbers didn't search their victims, they were "evidently novices at the business."

The Coming of the Mustang

Though it is long forgotten today, steamboat transportation once was big business on Texas rivers. Small stern-wheel and side-wheel steamers began appearing on Texas rivers in the 1830s and 1840s, and within a short time they made steam travel comparatively common for many Texans.

The arrival of the first steamboat at any riverfront community was of significant importance, for it indicated to all the world that the town had become a port. Thus the coming of the steamboat *Mustang* to Washington-on-the-Brazos on December 19, 1842, was a major event in the history of the town where the Texas Declaration of Independence had been signed only six years before.

The *Mustang* had been built in 1842 to serve as a ferry across Galveston Bay between the island city of Galveston and Virginia Point on the Texas mainland, but soon the vessel found itself plying the waters of the Brazos. Its destination became Washington-on-the-Brazos, for the town's merchants had offered a subsidy for the first steamboat that could reach that point.

One of the spectators who witnessed the arrival of the boat was John W. Lockhart, who wrote a remembrance of the event that was published in the *Galveston Daily News* on February 12, 1893. "As soon as the puffing of the boat was heard in the distance," Lockhart wrote, "there was an exodus from the town to the river bank." People from the country came on horseback, those from town on foot, all rushing to catch their first glimpse of the boat. One Alabama farmer brought his family in an ox cart, securing his animals to a wooden worm-style fence. Along with everyone else came most of the local Black slaves, crowding on the bluff overlooking the river with all the others to see what they could.

"The current was running swift and the boat, in order to take advantage of the eddy, steered for the opposite shore," the observer noted, "and when near us came across directly under us and eased up to the bank with so little noise as to cause one old lady to say, 'poor thing, it looks like it was tired.'"

In order to reduce the high pressure that had built up in the boiler, the steamboat engineer released the excess steam through a two-inch pipe that extended above the top deck of the little vessel. "It came with such force," Lockhart reported, "followed by the immense cloud of vapor," that the crowd, unfamiliar with steamboats, thought that the boiler was bursting. "It was immediately voted, without any preliminaries, that every man, woman and child should take care of themselves, and such a scattering was never witnessed." Men headed for large trees, while women with children clinging to their skirts made for whatever shelter they could find. The Black slaves started en masse for town.

The Alabaman's oxen, tethered to the fence, began making frantic efforts to escape. Finally tearing five or six panels of the wooden rails, the oxen stampeded with their cart behind them, followed by a pack of dogs barking at their heels. "They happened to head for town, right up the middle of the street, which was occupied just in front with the Negroes, who were seemingly doing their level best to escape the wreck and confusion," Lockhart related.

"In a very short time the ox cart procession had the whole street to itself and was gallantly escorted through" by the "whole pack of dogs," Lockhart reported, "and never stopped until it arrived safely at home in due time, four miles in the country beyond."

The 1842 Rise on the Brazos

Late spring and early summer bring high water to all the major Texas rivers. The flooding is caused principally by seasonal rainfall at the headwaters of the streams, although snowmelt contributes to the flow of some like the Canadian, the Pecos and the Rio Grande.

J. W. Lockhart came to the Brazos valley as a child in 1840, and two years later he witnessed one of its greatest floods. He and his family lived a short distance upstream from Washington-on-the-Brazos. During their initial two years in Texas, the family had experienced unusually dry conditions, and incongruously the weather where they lived remained clear and dry throughout the flood.

"This was a peculiar rise, in so much that there had been no rain up the river so far as we knew," Lockhart recalled fifty years later. Coming in late June, the floodwaters gradually rose half an inch to three inches a day until the lower valleys were all inundated despite the bright, sunny conditions.

The settlers around Washington-on-the-Brazos explained the rise by saying that it came from melting snow near the head of the river, but none of them knew where the Brazos actually began. "We had no communication with that far off region," Lockhart explained, adding, "We only surmised . . . that it headed somewhere in the Rocky Mountains." Today we know that the Brazos begins at the edge of the high plains of the Llano Estacado in West Texas.

Most settlers on the Brazos in the days of the Republic of Texas had no notion of what conditions were like in the western reaches of their country. "One who had been to the far off Cross Timbers [about one hundred miles] was looked upon as having performed a wonder in geographical feats and was considered quite a traveler," he explained. Everything west of the Cross Timbers, Lockhart stated, "was a sealed book, as much unknown to the inhabitants of Texas as the interior of Africa."

The floodwaters at Washington-on-the-Brazos reached so high into the cornfields at the Lockhart farm that J. W. Lockhart's father had to pick his corn while floating in a boat. The water covered the stalks all the way up to the ears.

Tremendous amounts of material drifted downstream during the flood of 1842. "Many buffaloes, wild horses and smaller game were seen floating down the river intermixed with driftwood, which consisted of immense cottonwood, oak, ash and pecan trees, green and fresh, going to show that there had been great erosion of the banks of recent date." This drift material made it almost impossible to cross the flood-swollen river with any safety.

Concluding his remembrance of the great flood, Lockhart declared, "There have been numerous floods since but none so great, according to my knowledge, as that of 1842."

Slave Hounds

During wartime people receive deferments from military service for a lot of varied reasons, but R. F. Harris of Chappell Hill, Texas, received his in the Civil War for an unusual one. It was on account of his pack of hounds.

Harris was a member of the local slave patrol. Known by black slaves as "paterollers," these were white men who went around with their dogs in the night to make sure the slaves were in their quarters and not wandering about. As the Civil War progressed, white people on the home front became almost paranoid with fear of an uprising among the slaves since most of the able-bodied white men were away fighting.

The members of white society in Chappell Hill saw Harris and his "pack of Negro dogs" as doing a "great service" in keeping the slaves "in subjection." Needless to say, the blacks did not necessarily share in this opinion.

Lewis Bonner, who was a slave on a Texas plantation, remembered, "The paterollers traveled from plantation to plantation during the nights with dogs, guns and bullwhips. They would sick the hounds on the slaves and when they would climb a tree," he remembered, "they would knock him out and the dogs would sometimes tear him up before they could get them off him."

Bonner, whose interview is preserved at the Oklahoma Historical Society, related that the slaves in going from one plantation to another after dark (when they were supposed to be home), would "carry plenty of pepper with them to rub on the bottom of their feet . . . so the dogs couldn't scent them."

Phyllis Petite, a slave in Rusk County, Texas, remembered in later life that one of the men from her plantation had tried to run away to freedom in the North, but "they caught him with bloodhounds and brung him back. The hounds nearly tore him up, and he was sick a long time."

One of the most vivid memories of what the slave hounds could do is found in the remembrances of Morris Sheppard, a slave over the Red River in Oklahoma. "One night a runaway Negro came across from Texas and he had the bloodhounds after him," Sheppard related to an interviewer about 1937. The fugitive's trousers were torn where the dogs had bitten his legs when he climbed too short a tree in the river bottoms. "He come up to our house and Mistress said for us Negroes to give him something to eat and we did."

Before long the Texan with his slave hounds came up and asked if anyone had seen his runaway slave. The mistress said that he was on the place, but then she asked him more than once who owned the fugitive so that she could buy him. She knew the punishment that undoubtedly awaited him in Texas and hoped to save him from the lashes of the bullwhip. "The man say he can't sell him," Sheppard remembered.

Since he was a slave himself, Morris Sheppard could only look on in sadness as the Texan took the runaway back south with shackles on his ankles. "I was sorry for him," he said, "because I knew he must have had a mean master" and he was unable to do anything to help.

Bump, Bump, Bump to Texas

Eliza Holman came to Texas in 1861, but not because she wanted to. She was a black slave and had no choice. Her trip from Clinton, Mississippi, to Decatur, Texas, was one she remembered all her life.

Half a century ago an employee for the Federal Writer's Project of the Works Progress Administration interviewed Eliza about her life experiences, and she talked about her trip to Texas as a slave. The interview is recorded in one of the four typewritten volumes of WPA-compiled Texas slave narratives now housed in the Manuscript Division at the Library of Congress in Washington.

One of Eliza's strongest remembrances of coming to Texas was the rough ride in the wagon. After eating breakfasts cooked on campfires, "it was bump, bump, bump all day long." The discomfort came because the roads were so rough, Eliza describing them as consisting of "rocks and holes and mudholes."

The ferry ride across the Mississippi River left a vivid impression. "We . . . drove on a big bridge," Eliza recalled, adding, "they floated that bridge right across the river."

All the way to Texas, Eliza listened to her master and mistress argue. The couple apparently found vocal disputes a means for venting their tensions during the course of the trip. Eliza's mistress seemed to be frightened by everything. Her husband repeatedly assured her, "The Lord is guiding us," but, the wife retorted time and again, "It is fools guiding, and a fool move to start." The former slave commented, "That's the way they talked all the way."

One night during the trip, the party camped beneath a huge tree at the side of the road. When they awakened the next morning, they all found themselves covered with masses of worms that had dropped down from the tree. "There were worms and worms and worms," Eliza remembered with distaste. "Millions of them came out of that tree." Her master identified the insects as army worms. His wife complained, "Why aren't they in the army then?" When travel conditions deteriorated, so did the arguments between Eliza's master and mistress, the enslaved woman continually taking in the verbal battle.

The feelings ran the highest when the wagons mired down in mudholes. The mistress would complain, "This is some more of your Lord's calls," to which the husband would reply, "Hush, hush, woman. You're getting sacrilegious." When the going got too rough, the slaves had to get out and walk or wait at the side of the road for the master to go for oxen to pull the wagons out of the mud.

When finally the wagons came free, the master would exclaim, "Thank the Lord," to which the mistress would counter instead, "Thank the men and the oxen." And thus the quarrels continued all the way to Decatur.

VII.

SOUTH TEXAS PLAINS

Mid-Nineteenth Century House of Sillar (Limestone Particulate), Guerra, Texas

Don Collins

The Journey of a Jacket

While participating in the translation to English of the Spanish-colonial Bexar Archives of San Antonio in the 1940s, historian Malcolm D. McLean found a surprising story from 1735 that documented the unexpected journey of a man's leather jacket.

In early summer 1735, Don Joseph de Vrrutia, the captain of the military garrison in San Antonio, sent his son to the military post at LaBahia near the Gulf coast to bring back some soap for his men. The supply in San Antonio had become exhausted, but there was plenty at the other location.

Joseph Miguel, the son, was delighted with the prospect of the trip. He went to the local blacksmith, Juan Banul, to borrow some harness for his animals and chanced to see his new leather jacket. Taking a fancy to it, Joseph Miguel asked if he could borrow it just long enough to make the trip to the coast and back, and Banul consented.

While at LaBahia, Joseph Miguel not only secured the needed soap, but he also looked over other merchandise available there but not at home. He spotted two pairs of ladies' shoes and some women's silk hose that he decided he wanted to bring back. (Who the garments were for, we don't know, but certainly one may suspect they were for a sweetheart.)

"I haven't a peso in my pocket," Joseph Miguel told Captain Costales, the LaBahia commander, who also was a storekeeper, "but I'd give the shirt off my back for those things."

"Your shirt, no," thought Costales, "but how about that fine leather jacket?" he asked. "Perhaps I could allow you something on it," he said, raising his eyebrows.

Joseph Miguel, who had only borrowed the jacket from Banul, lost no time in deciding what to do. He gave Costales the blacksmith's jacket for what he wanted.

Before Joseph Miguel set out for home in San Antonio with an oxcart load of the desired soap, Commander Costales gave the leather jacket to Francisco Diego de Miranda, one of the soldiers in the garrison. It chanced that Miranda had decided to accompany Joseph Miguel and the soap on the trip back to San Antonio, and quite naturally he wore his new jacket to the big city.

No sooner had Miranda in his new jacket arrived in San Antonio than he was met by a muscular stranger who blocked his way and roared out, "That's my jacket. Take it off!" The man was Banul, and he refused to accept any of Miranda's explanations about having received the garment from his commander. Banul knew the jacket and knew that it was his.

Finally the infuriated blacksmith took his demands to the San Antonio military commander, Don Joseph de Vrrutia. Realizing the complexity of the situation, the captain told Banul, "The jacket is no longer in our possession. Therefore, if you will tell me what you think it's worth, I'll pay you for it." Banul thought about the offer, but insisted, "It was specially made to fit me and I like it. Besides, I may need it to protect me if you order me out on campaign against the Indians."

Eventually the blacksmith consented to the commander's mediated resolution to the dispute, agreeing to accept twenty pesos compensation for the lost jacket. The sum was not small, for in 1735 it represented the equivalent of twenty days' work—enough to buy three horses. "Very good," said Captain Vrrutia as he settled the case, "That will be in trade, of course. I'll give you credit for that amount in my store." Banul was chagrined.

Illustrating how commerce in Spanish-colonial Texas operated, the leather jacket went from Banul to Joseph Miguel, from him to Captain Costales in LaBahia, and then on to Private Miranda, all the time without any money having to change hands. Clearly barter and not money was the principal means of exchange on the Texas frontier 276 years ago.

Eyewitness to the Alamo

Francisco Antonio Ruiz was there. He was an eyewitness. As the *alcalde* or mayor of San Antonio, he personally identified for Mexican general

Lopez de Santa Anna the bodies of some of the Alamo defenders after the makeshift fortress fell.

While the siege at the Alamo was going on, Mayor Ruiz's father, Jose Francisco Ruiz, was 150 miles to the east at Washington-on-the-Brazos. There he represented San Antonio as a delegate to the convention that formally declared Texas independence. No family was more closely involved in the Texas revolution.

In an account published in the 1860 *Texas Almanac*, Antonio Ruiz related that the Mexican army under the command of Santa Anna arrived in San Antonio at two o'clock on the afternoon of February 23, 1836. The forces occupied the town without resistance, for the Texan insurgents already had retreated to the fortified Alamo mission.

That very evening an exchange of gunfire began. Ruiz recalled that for thirteen days "the roar of artillery and volleys of musketry were constantly heard." He was in the city, and he heard the sound.

Early on the morning of March 6, the Mexican forces, which Ruiz estimated to number four thousand, advanced for a final assault on the 180-odd Texan rebels. "The Mexican army charged and were twice repulsed by the deadly fire of Travis's artillery," which Ruiz remembered sounding like a constant thunder. On the third charge the Toluca Battalion began to scale the fortified walls, but their toll was great. Out of 800 men, Ruiz reported only 130 survived. With the walls breached, however, the defenders soon fell to the overpowering numbers of Mexican troops. All the insurgent combatants were put to the sword.

The very morning the Alamo fell, Santa Anna called upon Ruiz for assistance. "He directed me . . . to accompany him, as he was desirous to have Colonel Travis, Bowie and Crockett shown to him."

Ruiz led the victor through the still smoldering shambles of the former mission, identifying the dead. "On the north battery of the fortress lay the lifeless body of Colonel Travis on the gun-carriage, shot only in the forehead," Ruiz related. "Toward the west, and in the small fort opposite the city, we found the body of Colonel Crockett. Colonel Bowie was found dead in his bed, in one of the rooms of the south side."

After Ruiz had satisfied this request, Santa Anna ordered him and other townspeople to carry the Mexican dead soldiers to the local cemetery. There were hundreds of them; Ruiz guessed the number to be

1,600. There was not enough room in the graveyard to hold them all, so Ruiz had some of the bodies thrown into the San Antonio River as a means of disposal.

As Ruiz conversed with the Mexican officers, he listened to them complain about their losses. He later remembered, "The gallantry of the few Texians who defended the Alamo was really wondered at by the Mexican army. Even the generals were astonished at their vigorous resistance, and how dearly victory had been bought."

Back at the Alamo, Santa Anna directed Ruiz to take a company of Mexican horse soldiers to bring in wood with which to burn the corpses of the defenders. "About 3 o'clock in the afternoon they commenced laying the wood and dry branches, upon which a file of dead bodies was layed." Then another layer of wood and corpses was laid, and so on until the work was done. "Kindling wood was distributed through the pile, and about 5 o'clock in the evening it was lighted."

The grisly details remained in Ruiz's memory the rest of his days. He wrote, "I was an eyewitness, for as *alcalde* of San Antonio, I was with some of the neighbors collecting the dead bodies and placing them on the funeral pyre."

Weird Dr. Weideman

"An eccentric character" was the way that Mrs. Mary Adams Maverick remembered 1840's San Antonio physician, Dr. Edmund Weidemann, and the description was an appropriate one.

A scholar who spoke several European languages, today he is best remembered for an incident in 1840 when he boiled the remains of two dead Indians in a big soap cauldron until the flesh cooked away from the bones so that he could mount the skeletons in his office. Then he dumped the liquid mess that was left over into an open irrigation ditch from which people downstream drew their drinking water. Needless to say, the act gained him few friends.

On one occasion Weideman discovered the loss of a watch. Suspecting one of his house servants, a man named Jose, the doctor waited for the man to confess the theft and return the property. After biding his time several days to no avail, the good doctor decided to take the matters into his own hands and try some "magic."

After inviting a party of his friends over to watch the fun, the physician moved his big soap pot up onto the flat roof of his house. Then he dressed in a figured robe and a sharply pointed hat. He truly looked the part of Merlin the magician of the Arthurian legends.

Weideman explained to all his household that he would ask each servant in turn to come up to the cauldron and dip his or her hands into the pot. Those of the guilty party would change color. With his guests observing the proceedings, the servants one at a time walked up to the big pot containing a mysterious liquid, thrust their hands down into the liquid, and withdrew them unchanged. Conscience-stricken Jose waited to the very last, just as Weideman had hoped, for he had surreptitiously added another ingredient to the mixture.

Jose finally approached his costumed employer, who looked like a magician if anyone ever did. "He . . . plunged in his hand," Mrs. Maverick related, "and when he withdrew it, lo, it was black!" In terror he confessed and immediately returned the missing timepiece.

Jose and all the other servants in the household concluded that the good doctor, who spoke in tongues they could not understand, undoubtedly had to be in league with the devil. Wiedman, however, seemed unconcerned, for nothing else ever disappeared from his home.

A German Texan's Tale

Traveling from Seguin to San Antonio in 1854, Frederick Law Olmstead and companions found themselves caught on the road at night with nowhere to stay. A visitor to Texas from the North, Olmstead was writing about his experiences for the *New York Times*.

The party sought shelter in a cabin occupied by recent German immigrants. "There were a man and his wife, with a son, and another single man, who came from Germany four years ago," Olmstead wrote for his readers. The immigrants had landed on Lavaca Bay and come inland to New Braunfels, where the single man found work first as a farm laborer and then later as a clerk in a San Antonio grocery store. The husband, who had been a shoemaker in Europe, had continued his Old World trade at New Braunfels.

At the end of two years of work, the two men pooled their resources to buy the one hundred-acre farm with an already existing cabin where Olmstead met them together with the wife and child. "The soil was extremely fertile, and the pasturage rank and nutritious," Olmstead reported, continuing, "their stock of cattle had been carefully watched, and, with the natural increase, now exceeded twenty head."

The home was what most impressed Olmstead, for the Germans had greatly improved the cabin that the preceding American settlers had thrown up. "They had taken up the rotten wooden floor of the American, preferring to it a hard earthen floor. They had repaired the roof, and, with a stucco which they had formed by mixing grass with calcareous clay, had made tight and smooth walls inside and out, doing all the work with their own hands." The traveler observed that the house was small but both snug and comfortable.

"And, are you glad you left Germany?" Olmstead asked the unmarried farmer.

"Oh, yes, very glad: a thousand times better here," he replied.

Then the traveler queried, "You can have more comfort here?"

To this he responded, "Oh, no; not so much. It is hard for a young man; he can have so little pleasure."

Here the German digressed to complain about the recreational outlets of the Americans living around him on the Texas frontier. "These American gentlemen, here in Texas, they do not know any pleasure. When they come together sometimes, what do they? They can only sit all round the fire and *speet*! Why, then they drink some whisky, or maybe they play cards, or they make great row. They have no pleasure as in Germany."

In response Olmstead next asked the immigrant, "Why, then, do you like it better to be here?" The answer was automatic:

"Because here I am free, In Germany I cannot say at all how I shall be governed. They govern the people with soldiers. They tried to make me a soldier, too, but I ran away."

The immigrant continued, "In three years I go back to Germany, I left a sweetheart there. I marry her and come back and have here my home."

"But," Olmstead asked, "Will they arrest you because you ran away and did not serve as a soldier?"

The immigrant, who had already applied for his American naturalization papers, had a ready answer: "Ah, no, for then I shall be a *citizen*!"

San Antonio's Bash for the "Sunset"

While Texas cities like Houston and Galveston had steam railways as early as the 1850s, San Antonio had to wait for two decades for the arrival of the iron horse. Until 1877 its economy stagnated, even though in its day the city had the second largest urban population in the state, because it suffered the impediment of all its freight having to go and come by animal-drawn wagons.

The isolation of San Antonio finally came to an end in 1877, when the steel rails of the Galveston, Harrisburg and San Antonio Railway reached there in mid-February. The working locomotives and flat cars that accompanied the laying of track were not viewed as the formal "first train," but when it did arrive the residents of the Alamo City pulled out all the stops in putting together a memorable celebration.

At noontime on February 19, 1877, railway company president Thomas W. Pierce headed a party of local dignitaries that traveled to a rendezvous point east of the city. There about 4:30 p.m. they met the first westbound passenger trail, the "Sunset," and boarded it. Already on the coaches were such special guests as Texas Governor Richard

B. Hubbard and the mayors of Austin and Galveston as well as two hundred other distinguished visitors from around the state.

Mayor James Henry French back in San Antonio headed a throng of well-wishers who greeted the "Sunset" as it pulled into the newly built Galveston, Harrisburg, and San Antonio depot. The crowd there grew so dense that he had to dispense with his formal welcoming speech and proceed with the festivities.

From the station French and the dignitaries led a torchlight parade of hundreds through the streets of San Antonio to Alamo Plaza, where the Menger Hotel formed the backdrop for a series of speeches. The scene illuminated by hanging Chinese lanterns on the front of the hotel, Governor Hubbard delighted the crowd with the prediction that the steel rails would enable the young men of East Texas to become husbands for the "rosy-cheeked maidens" of San Antonio. The audience cheered. A reception inside the Menger followed the speeches.

The next morning the activities again focused on the venerable hotel on Alamo Plaza, where Governor Hubbard was the chief attraction for a "mass of moving people" at a special governor's reception. Everyone seemed to want to shake his hand. Morning and afternoon local residents called at the hotel in their carriages in order to give out-of-town guests special tours of the Spanish missions and the San Pedro Springs. Throughout the day there were private parties all around the city.

On the evening of February 20, the activities shifted to Wolfram's Garden. There music, flag bedecked trees, and more lighted Chinese lanterns created a setting for additional speeches.

The celebration for the arrival of the railroad in San Antonio did not take place without problems, though most of them were of a good-natured sort. On the evening of the February 19, for example, while just about everyone at the Menger Hotel was either listening to speeches, attending receptions or otherwise partying, an unidentified prankster went from room to room switching the clothes of guests from chamber to chamber. Most of the guests laughed at the episode, but not everyone shared in the hilarity. One irate visitor came downstairs the next morning for his breakfast wearing a suit far too tight and a tiny little hat that would barely stay on his head, while he wore on one foot "a No. 5 Congress gaiter, and on the other a No. 12 cow hide boot." He, too, for a long time remembered San Antonio's bash for the "Sunset."

Santone Was Too Strenuous

One of the best known Texas telegraphers a century ago was a one-legged man now remembered as Peg, so-called from his wooden limb. He was as noted for his story telling ability as for his remarkable speed at the telegraph key. Peg had lost his limb in a railway accident. The railroad patched him up in one of its hospitals and gave him a fine wooden leg on the condition that he say nothing more about the matter.

Peg had an additional wooden leg for everyday use. Looking more like an ordinary broomstick than anything else, it was less ornamental but worked just fine. Peg was wearing this "everyday leg" on an occasion when he visited a vaudeville house in San Antonio back in the 1880s.

Having taken a seat near the rear of the theater, the telegrapher had been enjoying the typical vaudeville fare of music and comedy routines when an apparent drunken cowboy swaggered into the auditorium. Peg described him as having "two big guns strapped round his waist and a bowie knife that looked like a young sword."

After loudly ordering a bottle of champagne, the cowhand spotted the slightly elevated boxes with seats on either side of the stage and made for one of them. He climbed up the outside into the box and then proceeded to order three more bottles of champagne.

By this time the show had ground to a halt. A male singer on stage then began singing the next song, whereupon the drunk ordered him to stop. Ignoring the distraction, the singer continued, but the cowboy maintained his distractions by hammering on the box with a champagne bottle and by making other raucous noises.

Finally the singer stopped the show and asked if there were any law officer or anyone else in the house who would restrain the inebriated cowboy. No one volunteered, so the singer apparently decided that he would undertake the job himself.

After climbing most of the way up into the box, the singer was then bodily lifted upward and into the box by the burley drunk. "They dropped to the floor in a clinch, but as they fell I saw the cowboy had his knife in his hand," Peg related. After a minute or two of scuffling, the cowboy was seen to cram the singer's face into a wall, and then, as the telegrapher narrated, "he . . . rammed that big knife through him twice, and then, slamming it plumb through between the shoulders, he left it sticking."

At this point the audience made for the exit in one solid mass. "When I struck the sidewalk, I let out in good style and ran two blocks before I stopped," Peg said. Then he spotted a San Antonio policeman and breathlessly reported to him, "You had better go down yonder. A cowboy just murdered a man in the theater down there."

The officer calmly replied, "That's all right. . . . They have been killing that same man for two nights now. It's part of the show." Peg then realized that he had been "taken."

"Hold on," Peg interjected in telling the tale, "That story is not finished yet."

The next evening Peg, still wearing his everyday leg, returned to the theater to see what would happen that night. The show continued as it had the previous evening, but the mass exodus started earlier than he had expected.

"There was a big Dutchman near me and he stampeded at the first flash of the knife and took the whole tier of seats with him," Peg remembered. In the rush, his wooden leg got jammed into the seat and broken off. "Then they walked all over me, and I never saw a thing."

"When the dust settled," Peg continued, "they found me all spraddled out on the floor." The proprietor of the theater, according to the telegrapher, "acted pretty square." "He set 'em up two or three times, sent me home in a hack and next morning early they had a carpenter come around and fix my stem."

The excitement of San Antonio was too much for Peg, however, and the next day he left for El Paso.

"Santone was too strenuous for me."

A Texas Soldier of Fortune

"I am a soldier of fortune," wrote John S. Brooks, describing himself to his sister in a letter written from Texas in March 1836. Brooks indeed had devoted all his brief adult life to arms.

Born in 1814 in Staunton, Virginia, Brooks first served as a marine in the U.S. Navy. At that time, marines were soldiers who saw duty aboard warships. Having enlisted at Charlestown, Massachusetts, in September 1834, Brooks was noted in that year as "aged nineteen years, five feet, nine inches high, of a sandy complexion, red hair, blue eyes, and by trade or occupation a farmer." By February 1835, young Brooks had been promoted to the rank of corporal and was serving on the frigate *Constitution*, better known as "Old Ironsides."

Within a few months, in summer 1835, Brooks had become disenchanted with the marines. "My situation in the Marine Corps," he wrote on July 10, 1835, "is as disagreeable as it can be." He found himself unable to get along with his fellow soldiers. "The men . . . with whom I must necessarily associate . . . possess habits, passions and feelings with which I can never sympathize. . . . My life is perfectly miserable." Brooks applied for and received a disability discharge in autumn 1835.

Becoming freed from his marine obligations, Brooks didn't know what to do with himself. "What shall I do?" he asked in a letter to his brother. "Although I have procured my discharge, I cannot avoid entertaining the melancholy conviction that my prospects are as gloomy and uncertain as ever."

Finding no better options, Brooks determined to travel to Texas, where revolution was brewing against Mexico. He wrote to his father from New York on November 4, 1835, "Tomorrow morning I embark for the purpose of volunteering in the 'Rebel Army' of Texas."

Brooks safely arrived on the Texas coast, and at Velasco he volunteered for service in an army which was being formed for defense against an expected Mexican invasion. The Virginian wrote home to his father on December 23, 1835, "I am over the Rubicon and my fate is now inseparably connected with that of Texas. I have resolved to stand by her to the last." Joining forces under the command of James W. Fannin Jr., young Brooks went to Goliad, where he assumed responsibility for drilling approximately four hundred insurgent troops, most of them Americans.

John Brooks was so busy from his duties and so deprived of even the simplest comforts that he found just writing letters to be difficult. "I write amid the noise and confusion of a camp, sitting on the ground and holding the paper on my knee," he penned to his father on January 20, 1836.

Becoming a lieutenant, Brooks remained in the Goliad area until the surrender by Fannin following the Battle of Coleto on March 19 and 20, 1836. In this encounter, in which Fannin and his men were overpowered by a vastly superior force of Mexican troops, Brooks was badly wounded by a gunshot.

Dr. Jack Shackleford, a physician who cared for Brooks after the fight, later described for the Virginian's brother the injury which had befallen him. "He was in the battle of the Prairie on the 19th March," Shackleford wrote, "fought with a musket, . . . and received a very severe wound in the center of the left thigh which shattered the bone and caused great pain."

For a week the victors held Fannin's four hundred men prisoner at Goliad, the whole time being a nightmare of pain for Brooks. Dr. Joseph E. Field, who also attended the injured man, later wrote to his family: "His suffering was much more severe than is common in such cases in consequence of spasms in the muscles of the wounded thigh, which made him often pray for death."

The end of pain and imprisonment for Brooks and most of his fellow insurgents came on Palm Sunday, March 27, 1836. On that day the captors, under orders from Mexican president Antonio Lopez de Santa Anna executed all but a handful of Fannin's men. Palm Sunday was bloody in 1836.

On March 9, 1836, in his last letter to his friend, James Hargarty in New York, John S. Brooks predicted his own fate: "I will die like a soldier."

And . . . that he did.

Pork Steak on the Hoof

John C. Duval was one of the many young Americans who came to Texas in 1836 to join in its fight for independence. He was one of only a handful who escaped the Mexican army firing squads at Goliad that executed about 340 insurgents who had fought under James W. Fannin and then surrendered following the Battle of Coleto Creek.

During the weeks following Duval's escape, he walked northeastward up the gulf coastal plain through Mexican occupied Texas, expecting eventually to reach the security of territory held by revolutionary forces. Almost all this time he was alone and unarmed.

During his trek, Duval came across the home of a Texan settler, abandoned a few weeks earlier when its owner had fled the approaching Mexican troops. Having looked through the house fruitlessly for something to eat, the fugitive spotted a bed which, he noted, "looked very inviting to me after sleeping so long on the ground, [so] I concluded to accept the invitation and spend the night."

After resting well for a few hours, Duval was roused about midnight by an unexpected disturbance. "I listened attentively and soon ascertained that the noise was nothing but the grunting of several hogs that had taken up their quarters under the house whilst I was asleep." The house was built up on wooden blocks a foot or so above the ground, so the pigs had sufficient space for their accommodation.

As Duval lay in the bed, he realized that the swine could transmute into food for the coming days, so he began thinking about how he might catch one of the animals. Since the floor in the house was made from slabs of hand-hewn logs called puncheons that were held in place only by their own weight, he later wrote, "it occurred to me that I might bag one of these porkers by quietly lifting a puncheon immediately above the spot where they were lying and then quickly grabbing the first one I could get hold of."

Reluctantly climbing down from his comfortable berth, Duval listened carefully to the grunting to determine precisely where the hogs were bedded down. Then he quietly raised one of the thick planks.

"Thrusting my arm down through the opening," Duval remembered, "I felt around until my hand came in contact with the leg of a hog, when I suddenly seized it, and the row began." Somewhat to his dismay, the young American grabbed a hog that "was too large to be managed easily," and, as he later reported, "I . . . found it no easy matter to induce him to come up into my comfortable quarters." The hog, in fact, was so large an animal that it almost dragged Duval down through the broad opening in the floor. He knew, however, that if he let go, there would be no pork, for the disturbance had frightened away all the other swine.

"The idea of having no steak for breakfast gave me more than my usual strength," Duval reported, "and, at last, but not until he had cut me severely with his hard hoofs and rasped a good deal of the skin off my knuckles against the sharp edges of the puncheons, I drew him by 'strength and brutality' into the room and replaced the puncheon."

With the hog in the bedroom, Duval next had to dispatch the brute. Since he had no weapon and nothing sharper than a single blade from a small pair of scissors as a tool, Duval exited the house for the barnyard to look for some means for converting the hog into pork. Disappointingly the only implement found was a large wooden mallet used in splitting fence rails.

Returning to the room, Duval recalled, "I . . . made a determined assault upon the hog." The maul, however, was too heavy and awkward, so he found himself unable to wield a stunning blow to the pig. "Round and round the room we went for a quarter of an hour or more, the hog squealing all the while," until finally "I got a fair lick at his cranium, which brought him to the floor, where I finished him by continuous 'mauling.'"

The bloody deed completed, Duval tumbled back into the bed, waking up the next morning in broad daylight. He then butchered his hog with a broken piece of a drawknife he found at the house.

After building a fire, Duval cooked several pounds of the pork, eating all that he could manage for breakfast, and then carrying as much as he could as he continued his trek to freedom up the gulf coastal plain.

Arrested by Deaf Smith

Deaf Smith is best remembered by Texas history buffs as the man who burned the bridge at Vince's Bayou the day of the 1836 Battle of San Jacinto. On that day as one of Sam Houston's scouts, he headed the party that destroyed the bridge that blocked the retreat by both Texans and Mexicans at the battle in which Texas won its independence.

Swiss immigrant Charles Amsler remembered Deaf Smith for a different reason. . . . Smith arrested him!

Amsler immigrated to Mexican Texas in the summer of 1834, settling near Mill Creek in Stephen F. Austin's colony. In autumn 1835 he volunteered for the army which captured San Antonio from Mexican forces in the Texas revolution.

Amsler, like many Texas settlers, was not rich. Indeed he was poor. He had trouble assembling his equipment needed for military service, but, as he remembered, "I borrowed a worthless rifle of an acquaintance and set out." The firearm lacked a lock, the firing mechanism, so it was more for show than for utility, but it served him until he could get a better one a few weeks later.

After the Texan capture of San Antonio, Amsler volunteered as a member of the Texan expedition to the Rio Grande under Colonel James Grant and Colonel Francis W. Johnson. In March 1836 Grant's and Johnson's men were captured by Mexican troops and most killed, but health problems earlier intervened to save Amsler from the fate suffered by his comrades. "Becoming very sick on the march, I was left in the care of some Mexican rancheros two or three miles west of the mission of Refugio," he later said.

After several weeks of convalescence, Amsler became increasingly concerned about his family, but he was unable to go back to East Texas to check on them because he had no horse to ride and no money with which to buy one. "I made known my condition to some people living near the rancho who very kindly furnished me a horse, and I set out for home."

Late on the evening of his departure, Amsler passed through Goliad, where he secured provisions and then headed out again. Traveling an additional four or five miles, he camped for the night in a ravine a short distance from the road.

About two o'clock the next morning, the Swiss awakened, kindled a fire, and began boiling a small pot of coffee as he prepared for an early departure. "A man rode up and inquired where I was from," Amsler later related, and he told the stranger that he had come from the mission and was headed home to East Texas. "I am from San Antonio and am on my way to Goliad with dispatches for Colonel Fannin," the Texan commander there, the stranger said. "I am much fatigued and will rest a while with you."

The unidentified rider then dismounted, tied his horse, and joined Amsler in drinking a hot cup of coffee. They rested and chatted for about an hour, and then the stranger said, "Hell, my friend, we had better be traveling." As the Swiss went for his horse, the man asked, "Please bring my horse too."

During Amsler's absence the stranger picked up his gun, threw out the priming and poured water in the pan, making it unfirable. Then, as the unsuspecting Amsler returned with the two animals, "the agreeable stranger cocked his gun and presenting it at my breast, said, 'You are my prisoner.'"

Amazed and infuriated by the action, the Swiss demanded by whose authority and for what offense he was being arrested, to which the stranger replied, "By authority of Colonel Fannin and for stealing that horse." The Swiss assured the courier of his innocence, to which the stranger said, "My friend, I trust you did not steal the horse . . . but you are charged with having done so, and I shall take both you and the horse back to Goliad."

Toward Goliad they rode. After daylight began to glow, Amsler exhibited to his captor a certificate from his captain attesting to his good conduct during the Texan siege of San Antonio, but it was to no avail. Amsler also represented his penniless condition and his need to see his family in East Texas. The unidentified man seemed moved by the destitution of the Swiss and handed him two dollars, saying, "This is all the money I have—I can do without it and it may relieve you a little."

Amsler, still held prisoner, then asked the name of his generous captor. "He told me it was Smith—Deaf Smith!" he later remembered.

On arrival at Goliad, Smith turned over Amsler and the horse to Colonel James W. Fannin Jr., and a Mr. Conrad of Goliad, the rightful owner. The animal had been stolen by a third party, and Mr. Conrad had come to claim it. "After a short detention I was exonerated from the charge of theft and released," Amsler reported. "Now I set out for home on foot."

Amsler did make it home to find his family, and in later years he became a prosperous East Texas farmer.

Covered Bridge on the San Marcos

"It was one of the sensations we treated strangers to upon their introduction to Western Texas," wrote the editor of the *San Antonio Express* in 1869. His marvel was the covered bridge which once spanned the San Marcos River just west of Gonzales. To this day the cut stone piers that supported the old bridge still stand on either side of the San Marcos just above its confluence with the Guadalupe, but the story of the bridge goes back well over a century.

On the last day of 1854, the Texas Legislature granted a charter to Gonzales County planter John Mooney to erect a toll bridge across the San Marcos River on the Gonzales-Seguin Road. According to the statute, Mooney could place the bridge "at or within one mile of Benjamin Duncan's Ferry" and would have the exclusive right to operate any wagon bridges within four miles of that point on the San Marcos for the next twenty-five years.

Construction began in 1855 with the excavation of footings for two massive stone piers. Meanwhile, upstream crews began felling trees and hewing them into timbers for the wooden truss structure of the bridge and its two approaches. According to oral traditions, much of the labor came from black slaves.

After the wooden truss structure of the main span, approximately one hundred feet long, was built, it was covered with lumber sides and a shingle roof to protect it from the elements. This made it the only covered bridge in Texas in its day.

Upon the completion of the bridge, the *San Antonio Herald* on March 15, 1856, announced that its opening "will be very acceptable news to the public generally and the traveling community in particular," for it would eliminate problems in crossing the San Marcos during high water.

Early-day Texans considered the bridge to be a wonder. "Imagine a long narrow frame, boarded in on the sides, roofed overhead, and a floor underfoot, perched . . . 40 feet high over a fearful, swift, deep stream," wrote the editor of the *San Antonio Express* on July 14, 1869.

The San Marcos Bridge served social as well as transportation needs. Miss Mattie Harwood, a member of a pioneer Gonzales County family, many years ago recalled an occasion when she and friends on a picnic had to beat a hasty retreat from a thunderstorm to the protective shelter of the covered bridge. There the party spread its blankets on the roadway and enjoyed a meal uninterrupted by any travelers, the rain apparently keeping others off the roads. To this day stories are still told of the role of the bridge as a popular meeting place for sweethearts.

Purchased by the county in 1879, the San Marcos Bridge remained in service until it was replaced by an iron bridge in 1902. Some locals were glad to see the picturesque old covered bridge go, for they seem never to have felt very comfortable crossing its wooden span. As one Texan recalled, "The polite stage driver generally requested the gentlemen to walk over, while he undertook the perilous experiment of driving over the stage with the ladies inside, if there happened to be any on board."

He concluded, "We by far prefer a ferryboat—you wouldn't have to fall so far to reach the water."

A Sunday Sensation

Lindsey's Lone Star Saloon was not the usual haunt for Methodist pastor W. G. Rutledge of Eagle Pass, Texas, but that was where he preached on the evening of Sunday, October 9, 1892. The *Galveston News* carried a full report.

Rutledge had reached the end of a year's service as a missionary stationed in Eagle Pass, and he decided that as he prepared to leave the border town he would take the Gospel right into the den of iniquity, Captain Lindsey's Lone Star Saloon.

The proprietor had no objection to the missionary coming to hold services in his place of business, so on the appointed evening a crowd began to gather. Lindsey's establishment was no shabby tap room. The *News* described it as "a feature of the city, with its elegant fixtures, brilliant electric lights and all the attractions." Not only did people drink there, but they also gambled.

When Pastor Rutledge called the imbibers to order, he saw every chair in the barroom filled. He probably could hardly believe his eyes. Captain Lindsey, observing the proceedings, according to the newspaper report "looked dignified and sedate, and was an attentive listener."

"Handsome Dan" Bogard, the bartender, also gave Rutledge polite regard. When he was not otherwise occupied in "dishing out drinks to the thirsty comer," he reportedly gave "all attention" to the preacher's words. He did break his concentration, however, whenever a customer offered to "shake dice" for his drink.

Given the circumstances, the press reported, "There could be no complaint on account of lack of courtesy or lack of attention." The newspaper account continued, "The boys demonstrated that they could be gentlemen, even though the most of them had forgotten for years to say their prayers."

Pastor Rutledge's message was primarily an exhortation designed to impress his listeners, and it may have done some good. When he passed the plate for an offering following his message, the newspaper noted, "the boys chipped in freely and the crowd was dismissed."

During the course of the service a traveling salesman from Houston stumbled into the tap room, being greeted with Rutledge's words, "I beseech you." He opened both eyes wide, pinched himself to be sure he wasn't dreaming and then gracefully retreated to another bar.

Following the evening vespers, the saloon regulars made an expected run on the bar to refill their glasses and returned to their accustomed places around the tables. A customer from across the border in Mexico remarked that if this was the Texas style of entertainment, he didn't want to partake of it any further, while another borderer confessed to the others that he didn't think he had any more religion "than a cow."

Even so, Pastor Rutledge for the rest of his career in the ministry could tell his congregations the story of his witnessing his faith to the tipplers in the Lone Star Saloon.

VIII.

SOMEWHERE IN TEXAS

Keeping Texas Out

Not everyone wanted Texas to be part of the United States. In fact a lot of people were dead set against the annexation of the Texas Republic into the Union. This opposition had the effect of causing the Republic of Texas to persist as an independent nation for almost a decade before it became a state in the United States.

Through the years I'd read in textbooks about the opposition of Northerners to the entry of Texas into the Union, but the message had never "come home" to me until a short time ago.

Last winter in Boston I had the opportunity to return to some of my favorite haunts among the secondhand bookstores of the city. Up on the third floor of the old red brick Brattle Bookshop at 9 West Street, I found a stack of century-and-a-half-old Northern anti-slavery or abolitionist newspapers. They were full of boiling hot anti-Texas propaganda.

In the stack of yellowed newspapers, now collectors' items, I came across the July 21, 1837, issue of *The Liberator*. Published in Boston by William Lloyd Garrison, it was one of the most vocal of all the abolitionist papers. This particular issue focused on Texas matters, and it gave me new insights into the emotions of Northern opponents to Texas annexation.

In the summer of 1837, when the paper was printed, the U.S. government had just recognized the independence of Texas by a twenty-three to twenty-two vote in the U.S. Senate. Andrew Jackson had recently stepped down as president of the United States, and one of his final acts had been to appoint a diplomatic representative to the new Republic of Texas.

Most Texans would have been delighted if their country could have entered the American Union as a state, but when the U.S. Congress began considering this action, the "fat hit the fire" in Washington. Abolitionists in the North claimed that from the start the movement of Americans into Texas had been a plot by Southerners to extend black slavery westward from the United States into new territory. One of the writers in *The Liberator* described the purported Southern strategy by saying, "Texas is to be obtained first; and afterwards the aggressions on the Mexican territory will doubtless be repeated as often as a new area for slave labor is wanted."

The editors of *The Liberator* deplored the success of the Texas Revolution, seeing it only as a mechanism for expanding the domain of black slavery. A writer bemoaned the Texan victory over the Mexican army at San Jacinto as the "unfortunate defeat of the Mexicans, and the capture of the president of their republic, Santa Anna."

Through the summer of 1837, Northern abolitionists led a fight in Congress to prevent the annexation of Texas. In a typically fiery editorial, *The Liberator* asked its readers, "What are you prepared to do?" adding further in a rhetorical question, "To annex Texas to the Union, with its whips, chains, thumb-screws, and slavery?" The Northern writer concluded that the exclusion of Texas from the Union would "secure for you the gratitude of posterity, and the blessing of perishing millions."

Such opposition to Texas annexation was so strong that the effort to bring Texas into the Union in 1837 failed. In Congress, aging abolitionist and former president John Quincy Adams filibustered against Texas annexation for three weeks, successfully preventing the passage of the legislation.

Subsequently, New Englander Daniel Webster as U.S. Secretary of State delayed considering the matter for several more years. Eventually eight years would pass before the U.S. Congress again considered annexing Texas, finally voting in December 1845 to bring the Lone Star State into the Union.

When we Texans today proudly boast that our state was indeed an independent republic for almost a decade, perhaps we should think back and consider that the Texas Republic owed as much to the Northern abolitionists for its continued existence as a separate nation as it did to its own leaders.

John W. Bartlett's First "Wild" Indian

On October 24, 1850, John W. Bartlett met his first Texas Indian. He was on the road from Fredericksburg to El Paso.

A native of Rhode Island, Bartlett was the American commissioner for the U.S.–Mexican Boundary Commission from 1850 to 1853. He had been assigned to determine the official boundary between the two countries.

Earlier in life, Bartlett had helped found the American Ethnological Society and had written several books dealing with the cultures of Native Americans, but he had known only "civilized" Indians.

When Bartlett encountered Chipota, a Lipan Apache chief, he met his first "wild" Indian, and the encounter was one long remembered by both men. "Just as we were leaving camp," the commissioner wrote in his *Personal Narrative*, published in 1854, "an Indian mounted on a mule suddenly appeared from behind a clump of bushes."

Introducing himself in Spanish, the sixty-odd-year-old Chipota presented documents from a leather pouch that identified him and showed that he had recently signed a peace treaty with American authorities.

The heavyset chief, according to Bartlett, "had a pleasant, benevolent countenance, and . . . was well dressed in a suit of deerskin, with his bow and arrows slung across his back." The quiver for his arrows, the commissioner noted, was made from "the skin of the American leopard," apparently a jaguar.

Chipota told Bartlett that he and his band had been following the Americans for the past two days. Bartlett suspected that some of the old man's warriors might have been the cause for the loss of several mules that had disappeared, but he said nothing. He did, however, need replacements for the missing animals.

The Lipan chief knew enough about the white men's ways to realize that when they met it often was customary for them to share drinks. "Finding no proffer of such civilities, he gave me to understand that he would not object to a glass of whiskey," Bartlett wrote. The straitlaced New Englander replied that he didn't have any alcohol, but that if the chief would accompany the party to its next camping place, he could offer him a shirt and something to eat.

"I asked him to take a seat in my carriage," a fine Rockaway coach with luxurious appointments. "He accepted with a delight that showed itself in spite of his endeavors to maintain his gravity," Bartlett related.

"He manifested much curiosity respecting all he saw, for the carriage was well filled with a variety of knick-knacks which were new to him."

Among the items that Chipota spotted was a handheld telescope. Bartlett wrote: "The instrument was adjusted, and a distant tree pointed out, which he was told to look at with the glass. His credulity had been over tasked, and it was hard to convince him that it was the same far-off tree."

Finding that Chipota's band had excess mules, Bartlett asked him to bring them in so that the Americans might buy some to replace the ones which had been lost. "I . . . offered them ten dollars each, or goods to that amount," but the chief seemed uninterested.

In the afternoon Chipota departed for his own camp, only to return in the evening with a handful of his tribesmen. "As they showed no inclination to leave, we were obliged to give them a supper, after which they asked permission to remain all night with us." The commissioner reluctantly consented to the request, on the condition that the Lipans slept by their own fire outside the white men's camp.

"The night was rather cool," Bartlett remembered, "and day had scarcely dawned, when I was aroused by a tap at the window of my carriage." Outside he saw old Chipota, shivering from a cold night on the ground.

When the commissioner opened the door to his coach, the chief chattered through his teeth, "Mucho frio—poco de viskey," or "Very cold—a little whiskey."

"I was compelled again to deny the old man, but compromised the matter soon after by giving him a bowl of hot coffee," Bartlett said.

For Chipota the coffee must have been a poor substitute for what he wanted because that morning he departed camp, still refusing to sell Bartlett the mules that he needed.

The First Day for a New Teacher

Keeping school in Texas during the 1850s was no simple task, especially for teachers newly arrived in the state. Fortunately one such lady, whose identity now is unknown, left us an account of her first day in a Texas school which subsequently was published in the August 1853 *Putnam's Monthly Magazine.*

The anonymous teacher described her schoolhouse as a rough log cabin set in a grove of oaks, a pleasant location "were it not infested with legions of gnats, whose bite for venom would do credit to larger insects." The building had a doorway and a single window without sash or glass. Lack of light or ventilation presented no problems; the gaps between the logs admitting fresh air in larger quantities than desired.

Entering the classroom for the first time, the schoolmistress rang her handbell to summon her child scholars. "They came with a whoop and halloo, twenty-five in number," she noted. They ranged in age up to twenty years old.

The pupils thronged around the teacher, for new people in the community were considered curiosities. Some of the boldest of the girls fingered her dress, wanting to know the price she had paid for the calico. "Others plucked the artificial flowers from my bonnet," the teacher wrote, "and arranged them into bouquets for themselves."

The teacher found the names of her charges to be more than surprising. "I was struck with the love of the high sounding and romantic manifested by the parents," she wrote, noting such names among her pupils as Cleopatra Aletha and Phedora Constantia.

No sooner had the class day begun than a swarm of a dozen or so wasps swooped down from a rafter. Teacher and children precipitously fled the cabin. "The wasps not finding anyone to molest, soon flew away, and we returned to our places," she later wrote.

Back in the classroom, the new schoolmarm began observing that the children were paying more attention to a rafter above her head than to her lesson. Looking up, she spied "an enormously long snake, coiling and uncoiling himself with the utmost sang-froid." Terrified by the reptile, "flight was our only alternative," she wrote. "Setting the example, I was followed by my twenty-five pupils, leaving his snakeship and the nest of young wasps undisputed monarchs of the building."

By now it was noontime, so teacher and children took a lunch break while a man dislodged the serpent using a burning piece of cotton attached to the end of a long pole. In their lunch pails, the pupils found the ever-common Texas cornbread and bacon, quenching their thirsts with drinks from a nearby spring. After their meal, one group of children began playing by imitating the behaviors that they had seen among their elders at a recent camp meeting. "Their shouts, groans and amens made the primeval forest echo," according to the teacher.

Returning to the log schoolhouse after the break, one of the little girls, Cleopatra Alethea, asked the teacher, "Please put me in potash." "I have none," replied the teacher, asking, "Why . . . do you want to be flayed alive in potash?" With big dark eyes opened wide, the girl looked up confused at the schoolmistress; then she pointed in her spelling book at a column of words that began with the word *potash*. "The mystery solved, I forthwith overjoyed her little heart by advancing her to the desired column," the teacher said.

The day drew to its close and the children headed home, full of stories for their families about their new teacher. After the classroom fell silent, the young woman turned her own tread toward home, pondering the mountain of ignorance that she had been hired to dispel. "Amused with the oddity of my situation," she wrote, "I strayed musingly homeward, so absorbed that I narrowly missed being stung by a tarantula in the path."

Thus ended the first day for the new teacher.

Trapped in a West Texas Well

Never had Bob endured such misery as he did at the bottom of a shallow well on a West Texas sheep ranch about a century ago. Bob was a fellow countryman of English cowboy J. H. Pollock, and the latter narrated the story of Bob's close brush with death in his autobiography, *The Unvarnished West*.

Throughout West Texas water wells often provide the few dependable sources of moisture for vast tracts of semiarid pasture. These wells, as sources of life, at the same time may constitute death traps. The victims of the wells usually are insects and small animals that fall into them as they seek drinking water, drowning because they can't escape. When a rancher fails to clean such a well, it becomes what Pollock aptly described as "an evil-smelling pit of corruption." Even this is an understatement.

Pollock's friend, Bob, a former trooper in the First Royal Dragoons in the British army, unknowingly stumbled onto an abandoned hand-dug well one day while seeking some lost sheep. "He . . . was scanning the horizon more carefully than watching where he put his feet," Pollock commented.

The well had been covered with boards to prevent livestock from falling down inside, but the lumber had rotted and "so proved no protection to an unsuspicious pedestrian."

Bob fell right into the well, which fortunately was only nine or ten feet deep. He was unhurt by the fall but was trapped underground, unable to climb out. Complicating the situation was the fact that the well held between four and five feet of water combined with untold accumulated decaying animal carcasses.

"There he was, standing several feet below the level of the ground," Pollock wrote, "with this putrid water almost up to his mouth." The sun beamed down on bareheaded Bob, leaving him thirsty to the extreme but unable to drink. Bob shared the reeking water with the bodies of opossums, raccoons, skunks and rats, all of them bobbing up and down in the liquid with "every movement of his limbs or body."

The situation was more than just disagreeable. It was downright dangerous. The well might easily have become a death trap for the cowboy as it had for the other animals. Making the man's situation even more precarious was the location of the well, far back among some low hills away from the usual paths of travel across the ranch. "The thought that he too might soon become a member of that prairie cemetery in which he found himself cannot have added much to his comfort," Pollock observed.

The Englishman's salvation came in the form of a party of cowboys that chanced to be riding through the remote back area of the ranch. They were attracted to the well, Pollock reported, "by the stream of profanity and bad language proceeding therefrom."

Finding Bob in the bottom of the well, only his head protruding upward from the awful smelling corruption, "they drew him out of his malodorous seclusion."